Fundamentals of
Production/Operations Management
Third Edition

Fundamentals of
Production/Operations
Management

Third Edition

Harold E. Fearon
William A. Ruch
Vincent G. Reuter
Department of Purchasing, Transportation, Operations
Arizona State University

C. David Wieters
New Mexico State University

and

Ross R. Reck

WEST PUBLISHING COMPANY
St. Paul • New York • Los Angeles • San Francisco

Copyediting: Susan Jones
Typesetting: Century Design
Cover: Pete Thiel

Library of Congress Cataloging-in-Publication Data
Main entry under title:
Fundamentals of production/operations management.
        Bibliography: p.
        Includes index.
        1. Production management. I. Fearon, Harold E.
TS155.F83 1986   658.5   85-20349
ISBN 0-314-93177-5

Contents

Figures, Exhibits, and Tables

Figures

Exhibits

Tables

Preface

When we originally wrote the first edition of this book in 1979, we did it out of two convictions: (1) a concise treatment of the production/operations management function was needed as a means of giving college students and persons in executive development programs a basic understanding of the area, and (2) the teaching of production/operations management need not use a highly-mathematical approach, which tends to divorce the student from the problems generally faced by the manager. Instead, it should treat POM in a way which will enable an easy grasp of the fundamentals. If more detailed information on any of the subjects discussed in this book is needed, the end-of-chapter references indicate where it can be obtained.

Those who have used this book in its two earlier editions over the past six years indicate that it does convey to the student, in an understandable manner, (1) the basic concepts of POM, (2) the substantial professional opportunities in the area, and (3) the challenge and excitement in managing production/operations.

As organizations around the world intensify their efforts to increase productivity and become more competitive, the techniques in POM are refined and extended into new areas. This is a continuous process; the student and manager must be aware of the changes taking place. The newer developments in POM have been incorporated within the framework of the functional approach in this third edition. We hope the users find it to be as direct and straightforward as did those using earlier editions.

Special thanks go to Mrs. Patricia Welch, Administrative Assistant in the Department of Purchasing, Transportation, Operations at Arizona State University for facilitating the manuscript preparation. The authors, of course, take full responsibility for any errors which might appear in the final product.

The Authors

Fundamentals of
Production/Operations
Management
Third Edition

Chapter 1

The Production Function

Virtually all the products and services we enjoy are created for us. Our economic system uses available inputs or natural resources and combines these with another important input—the effort, skills, and knowledge of labor. The result is an array of goods and services, such as automobiles, health services, roads, electricity, golf clubs, police protection, food, and movies, available for distribution. Each of these products or services requires *inputs* that are *converted* into usable *outputs*. The management of the conversion process of transforming inputs into outputs is the essence of production/ operations management.

This book will describe the fundamentals of those areas that make up production/operations management (POM). It will discuss the importance of each area and show how the various functions fit together to make up an effective, efficient production system. It will not attempt to provide all the details and nuances of each area. In-depth discussions of the tools, techniques, and issues in POM can be found in many more-extensive and more-advanced texts, some of which are listed at the end of each chapter.

Why Study Production/Operations Management?

Production/operations management has suffered in the past from a bad reputation among college students. It seemed to lack the glamour of marketing and finance and had less inherent interest than personnel and organizational behavior. Some people would say, "I don't plan to work in a factory, so why should I study production?" There are several answers to that question.

First, as we shall soon see, production/operations management applies to every organization in every industry and in every sector of our economy.

1

Although its roots are in manufacturing, the techniques can be applied across a broad spectrum of situations. Indeed, some of the most exciting and rewarding opportunities today involve the application of ideas and models traditionally associated with manufacturing to such service industries as banking, recreation, and food services and even to government agencies.

Second, many students find that the field of production/operations management can be more intriguing and exciting than their initial impressions led them to believe. Production is where the action is in most business firms. The operation and control of the production process—whether producing hamburgers, automobiles, or insurance policies—is demanding work, requiring talent, skill, and a desire to get the job done right and on time. The people who manage the direct-work process derive great satisfaction from seeing the results of their efforts in terms of goods shipped and services delivered.

A third reason for studying production/operations management relates to the laws of supply and demand. At present, more opportunities than graduates exist in this field. As the need continues to grow in service industries for people who can plan, schedule, and control, the market for POM graduates will remain stable. In many universities, POM graduates receive more job offers at higher salaries than any of their colleagues.

Not everyone should become a POM major; however, all business students should be aware of the nature of each of the major subfunctions of business. The fourth reason for studying POM, then, is to complete an education that otherwise would be seriously lacking. Knowledge of the special problems and issues in POM will enhance the effectiveness of the accountant, the marketing manager, the financial analyst, or the personnel specialist. An integrated-systems approach based upon an understanding and appreciation of all business functions is the goal of every organization.

The Production Function

Every organization has a production function, just as it has a finance function and a marketing function. Finance is concerned with the acquisition and use of funds, while marketing is focused on selling and distributing the products and services. The production function is the third side of this triangle, for it uses the funds acquired by finance to buy raw materials, machines, and labor and converts these into products and services that marketing can sell.

Inputs

Part of the production function concerns the acquisition of inputs, as illustrated in figure 1-1. Any product or service that is created requires some combination of materials, machines, and people. General Motors employs hundreds of

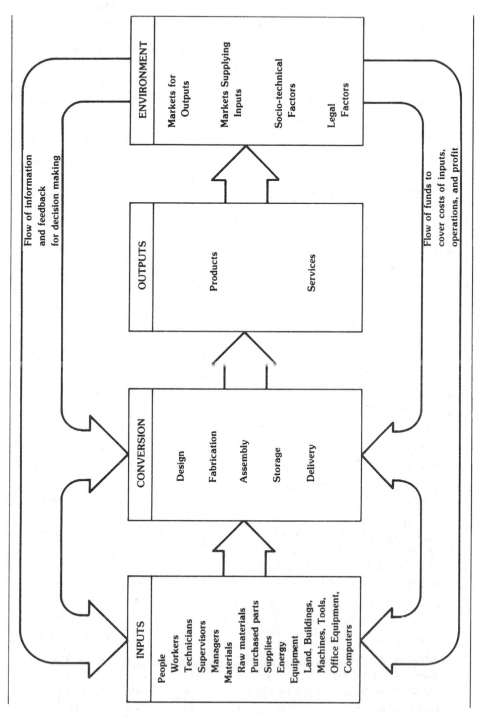

Figure 1-1.   The Production Function

thousands of people, ranging from unskilled or semiskilled workers to top executives. They use billions of dollars worth of plants, machines, and tools and purchase materials (steel, glass, fabric, plastic, etc.) at the rate of more than 100 million dollars a day to produce the millions of cars the world wants. One of their suppliers, Small Parts, Inc., employs about 50 workers and a dozen machines to make tiny metal parts out of strip steel. The two firms are vastly different in size and scope, yet each draws from the same basic categories of inputs to produce its unique outputs.

The list of inputs is almost endless. The people category includes unskilled, semiskilled, and skilled workers; clerical personnel; secretaries; technicians; supervisors; professionals (doctors, teachers, etc.); part-time students; supervisors; engineers; artists; accountants; and executives.

Similarly, materials and equipment come in all forms, sizes, and shapes. A critical part of the production function is the acquisition of the proper raw materials, tools, machines, and other supplies and equipment to permit the efficient and effective operation of the firm. The lack of even low-cost parts can idle hundreds of men and their equipment.

Acquisition of capital inputs (land, buildings, and machinery) is generally done at high levels in the organization. A firm frequently enlists specialists in real estate, finance, law, and capital budgeting to work as a team to decide on locations and equipment for new facilities. Large motel chains, fast food firms, and many retail houses typify this situation. Where these acquisitions are less frequent, a firm may designate key executives as an ad hoc committee to work with outside consultants to reach a decision.

Acquisition of people inputs is the primary responsibility of the personnel department. Recruiting, interviewing, testing, selecting, hiring, placing, evaluating, compensating, and terminating are subfunctions of this activity. The personnel department provides a service to the rest of the firm by arranging for the proper manpower when and where it is needed. Trained personnel specialists can perform this task more effectively and efficiently than could each department duplicating these functions.

Both manufacturing firms and service organizations (including government) rely on purchasing managers to obtain material inputs, including raw materials, purchased parts, and supplies. Purchasing managers, skilled in the techniques of buying and knowledgeable about the products for which they are responsible, buy the proper raw materials for a hospital or a restaurant; this task is no less important than in a manufacturing firm.

The purchasing department staff may constitute a small percentage of the organization's personnel, yet it exerts a major influence on the profit-making ability of the firm, due to the dollars involved. Chapter 5 examines this purchasing function in depth.

Conversion

Merging the time and place and transforming the form of the inputs to make them more usable and accessible to customers is the conversion process. The customers may be final consumers, or they may be other business firms in the chain between natural resources and final users. Because the time and place aspects of the output are handled primarily by the marketing and distribution functions of the firm, the emphasis here will be on form of the output—that is, the creation and production of goods and services.

A useful distinction can be made between the *technology* of transformation and the *methodology* of transformation. Technology refers to the scientific principles applied to convert inputs to outputs; often, this is unique within an industry. For example, the petroleum industry applies its technology—derived from chemistry, physics, hydraulics, and other sciences—to convert crude oil into gasoline, aviation fuel, asphalt, tar, paint, and many other salable products. No other industry uses exactly the same technology.

A dairy, on the other hand, begins with raw milk and produces whole milk, skim milk, butter, cheese, ice cream, and other products. The technology in a dairy is quite different from an oil company, yet the processes are similar enough to allow application of much of the same methodology. The problems of scheduling, controlling, storing, shipping, and generally *managing* the two processes are similar.

This text will concentrate on the methodology of transformation and will draw examples from specific technologies. Principles of scheduling can be discussed and then applied to either a machine shop or the receiving ward of a hospital. Techniques of inventory control apply equally well to inventories of fresh vegetables or auto parts. Although the examples will vary, the reader is encouraged to apply the principles and techniques in each chapter to as many organizations or processes as possible to facilitate understanding. Laundries, libraries, fraternities, bicycle repair shops, government bureaus, real estate agencies, car washes, liquor stores, banks, barber shops, medical offices, auto agencies, and even universities have transformation processes to which the tools and techniques of POM can be applied.

Outputs

It is easy to say that the output of an automobile manufacturer is automobiles, the output of a restaurant is meals, and the output of a university is graduates. Very few firms, however, produce only one output. The auto manufacturer, for example, produces an array of body styles, colors, and optional equipment. It also may produce trucks, industrial vehicles, refrigerators, and railroad engines. In addition to the physical products, the firm also may provide many services, such as warranty repair, delivery, setup, financing, and training.

The total array of outputs of the firm should be considered, because two outputs may complement or supplement each other to the firm's advantage. In other cases, outputs may conflict to the detriment of profitability and effectiveness. For example, a firm that produces razor blades may benefit if it also produces razors, but a travel agency probably would not benefit from also selling TV sets.

When manufacturing a product, the firm begins with raw materials, feeds them through a conversion process, and ends up with a finished product ready to sell. In the decision-making process, however, the time sequence of the steps is reversed. The firm begins with the design of the output, forecasts sales, and then uses these specifications and projections to set up the conversion process and acquire inputs. Thus, the desired output is the goal from which all other decisions are derived.

Environment

Every business operates in an environment that provides markets for the products and services it produces, as well as markets from which the firm buys inputs. In addition, the environment provides socio-technical and legal constraints and guidelines within which the firm must operate if it is to be law-abiding, socially responsible, and successful.

To make the model complete, two feedback loops are necessary. First, the sale of goods and services produces the flow of dollars back to the firm to purchase additional inputs, to pay operating costs, and to generate profits for owners. Second, a constant flow of information from the environment to the firm allows management to employ new technology and respond to changing needs and desires of customers.

Providing Services

Production and operations management often is mistakenly associated only with manufactured goods. Indeed, today's instruction in POM traces its roots to college courses titled "Production Management," "Manufacturing Management," and "Factory Management." Yet the addition of the word *operations* signifies that many of the concepts originally developed in and for the factory apply equally well to service firms, not-for-profit organizations, and government agencies.

All nonmanufacturing organizations perform the same basic functions. They acquire inputs of people, materials, and equipment; convert them into outputs (in this case, services); and deliver them to their customers. This is true for a bank, hospital, public utility, restaurant, counseling service, state park, military base, barber shop, book store, trucking firm, library, health club, and, of course, a university.

As with manufacturing, the size and scope of the service firm and the types of services produced determine the relative importance of POM functions. In a health club, for example, the types of services to be offered must be designed and the hours of operation set. Probably the club will be capital intensive, with a large investment in equipment and relatively few employees. Inventories of raw material would be small, consisting mainly of supplies. Location and layout decisions would be important, but forecasting, planning, and scheduling for the club could be the most critical.

Other service firms would have a different balance. In a restaurant, for example, purchasing and inventory control would be critical. In this case, "raw" material means exactly that!

With services accounting for a larger and larger portion of business activity, it is important that principles and practices that have proved beneficial in manufacturing be used to make the provision of services more effective and efficient. The task of scheduling patients in a hospital emergency room, for example, can be accomplished by using the waiting-line method; just as this system is used to schedule jobs in a machine shop. Assigning costs to waiting patients is more difficult than for materials, but it can be done. The challenges may be greater because of the less tangible nature of services, but the potential rewards make the effort worthwhile.

Production/Operations Management and Other Business Functions

The production/operations function interacts closely with each of the other key functions of any organization. In concert, these functions—and their interactions—determine the success or failure of an organization. One company may be called a "marketing organization"; another an "accounting firm"; yet each must integrate the functions of finance and accounting, human resources (personnel), marketing, and production/operations. Although often treated separately for purposes of analysis and study, the functions are merged into a total system in an organization; dividing lines between functions are not easy to see in the real world. It is important, therefore, not only to examine the production/operations function but to keep in mind critical interactions with other functions.

Production/operations employs the capital resources acquired by the finance function. It converts funds into equipment, tools, facilities, and inventories to produce products and services. The decision to replace an old machine with a new one is not solely a technical decision nor a financial one; it must be a combination of the two. The decision is made using capital budgeting analysis based on information concerning the capacity of the machine and its relationship to other phases of the production process; for example, the new machine may produce at a higher speed, but it may also require more maintenance, produce more scrap, or use more energy.

Accounting data are needed to make this equipment decision as well as most other decisions in the production/operations function. Inventory policies, for example, depend upon the value of the item in stock. The knotty problem of determining the value of the in-stock unit, either purchased or manufactured internally, depends on sound accounting principles applied through an accurate, timely management information system to evaluate the effects of past production/operations decisions and to provide input to future decisions.

Production/operations cannot function without people. The human-resources function recruits and trains workers to fill positions within the production process according to the job design and skill assessments performed by work-study analysts. As changes—involving overtime, adding a shift, employing newer technologies, or redesigning the product—are made in the production process, they must be coordinated with the human-resources function. To ensure a smooth transition as the change takes place, this coordination should occur during the planning phase.

The interaction between production/operations and the marketing function is both complex and critical. It is simplistic to say that marketing sells what production produces or vice versa. Actually, marketing research gathers information that guides the design or redesign of products and services. A marketing forecast of sales potential must be integrated with a production forecast of capacity to provide a realistic production schedule. Marketing promotes and sells; production produces and delivers. If any link of that chain is weak, the entire organization suffers. Many cases can be found of firms with good production *and* good marketing functions that have failed because of a lack of coordination between the two.

History of Production/Operations Management

Production/operations management began when the first crude tool was produced. In the ensuing years, we have reached the point where nearly everything we touch is a manufactured or processed product. Improvement in *performing* manufacturing tasks has been a gradual, if not consistent, trend. But the systematic *study* of production is a relatively recent phenomenon, confined mainly to the last 200 years and concentrated in the last 80.

We think of mass production as a twentieth century concept, yet assembly lines were in use in the early fifteenth century. Venetian shipbuilders equipped their fighting galleys by towing them through a water channel between warehouses where the provisions and equipment were stored. They eventually reached a production level of equipping a ship every 36 minutes.

In the fifteenth century, no mass markets existed, nor were there advertising, distribution networks, or other support services. Measurement technology and manufacturing methods were not yet sufficiently precise to produce interchangeable parts. Mass production, therefore, was found only in rare, isolated instances; manufacturing at this time was performed predominantly by independent craftsmen.

Factories began to appear in the early eighteenth century in the textile industry and later were built to accommodate other types of manufacturing. In 1776, Adam Smith described, in *The Wealth of Nations*, the subdivision of labor employed in manufacturing pins. Later scholars, such as Charles Babbage, developed and refined Smith's theories of organization of work. During the two centuries from 1700 to 1900, the industrial revolution flourished, and students of this emerging field attempted to describe the new developments and provide theoretical foundations for existing practices. Only in the twentieth century have scholars been able to develop theories based upon research and experimentation and then to implement them in business.

Frederick W. Taylor was one of the first people to study business using a scientific approach. In the early 1900s, business knowledge was not yet organized into principles. Taylor studied business by beginning with basics, experimenting, and adding building blocks to form a cogent body of knowledge. Many of the principles of management he developed are being taught and used effectively today.

Other pioneering scholars such as Frank and Lillian Gilbreth advanced Taylor's work in motion and time study. Industrialists like Henry Ford applied these principles to mass production and built empires from which flowed manufactured goods that many could afford.

The early twentieth century was a period of rapid growth and change. Factories were becoming efficient, if not yet humanistic. Upton Sinclair described the evils of this capitalistic system in an expose of the meat-packing industry titled *The Jungle*. The working conditions he described were horrifying, but rather than repelling people from capitalism, his writings led to government regulations (such as the Pure Food and Drug Act) and fueled the labor movement to develop powerful industrial unions to protect workers' rights. Before the middle of this century, human relations research had begun to develop principles of effective utilization, rather than exploitation, of workers.

Many tools and techniques developed in the first half of this century have enhanced the efficiency and effectiveness of business organizations. In 1915, F. W. Harris developed the economic order quantity formula that now is a fundamental concept in inventory control. A decade later, several individuals, including H. F. Dodge, H. G. Romig, and W. A. Shewhart, applied probability theory to quality control and introduced the concept of assessing quality based on a random sample. Waiting-line theory was born, and work sampling first was applied. On other fronts, the first experiments in work-group behavior were laying foundations for human-relations and organization-behavior theories.

The decade of the 1940s and World War II produced the most concentrated manufacturing effort yet known. Operations research (OR) teams found ways to better utilize severely limited resources to fill the greatly expanded needs caused by the war. When the war ended, the military outputs were changed, but the new OR techniques had found a permanent place in industry.

Perhaps the single most important technological advancement in the recent history of business is the computer. Applications in accounting, finance, marketing, and personnel abound, as they do in POM. The various tasks of scheduling and control always have been performed, but the computer now permits complex algorithms routinely to be applied in situations where judgment and guess previously prevailed. Material requirements planning (MRP), a technique that determines when and how much material to order, is becoming an invaluable managerial tool, but it cannot be employed effectively without a computer because it involves a vast number of calculations.

Just-in-time (JIT) inventory systems, popularized in Japanese manufacturing firms, rely on computerized scheduling of raw materials to arrive just as they are needed in production, thus eliminating costly levels of inventory. (MRP, JIT, and other systems are described in more detail in chapters 4 and 6.)

Recent developments in minicomputers are making it possible for many small manufacturing companies to take advantage of computer control techniques in manufacturing. In fact, the very definition of what constitutes a minicomputer is becoming difficult to determine. Minicomputers originally were classified as small computer systems with limited storage capacity and functional capability; they often were used to support only a single application. With the explosive growth in computer technology, however, these so-called minicomputers have capacities and functions that equal or surpass the larger data-processing equipment of just a few years ago, and a wide assortment of manufacturing software support for the minicomputer user now is available.

The microprocessor—a computer on a chip—is another modern technological development that has far-reaching implications for the management of production systems. Microprocessors are designed to perform a single application but are inexpensive and can be preprogrammed to perform a wide variety of logic functions; consider, for example, the capabilities found in video games and hand-held calculators. The major difference between a microprocessor and a small computer is that there is limited ability to reprogram a microprocessor: all the programmed logic is predetermined and actually designed into the physical circuitry itself. Microprocessors are being developed to support new applications of industrial robots and many of the functions performed in computer-aided design and computer-aided manufacturing (CAD/CAM) systems.

In addition to minicomputers and microprocessors, other related tech-nologies may impact production planning and control systems. These include magnetics (i.e., the magnetic stripe used on the back of bank cards); optical reading of numeric and alphabetic printed data; and light scanning or laser sensing devices like those used in supermarket checkout systems and de-partment store point-of-sale terminals. In an operations environment, such devices may be used for data collection in receiving, storeroom, and shipping operations.

The Future of Production/Operations Management

Although predicting the future is risky, certain basic trends exist in POM and probably will continue in the foreseeable future. The first of these is the increase in the level of sophistication of technology, both in the products themselves and in the processes used to manufacture them.

Plastics and other synthetic substances have replaced natural products, such as leather and cotton, in many applications. As a new basic product is created, existing industries change and new industries emerge. Oil companies become petrochemical firms, and electronics firms are established to produce items that did not exist a decade ago. The advent of the electronic watch even has led some unlikely companies into the jewelry business. And we stand on the threshold of an entirely new industry in biogenetics.

Just as bulldozers now substitute for a pick and shovel, lasers will be commonly employed in such diverse industries as mining and medicine. Solar-powered equipment will alleviate demands and restraints on other energy-distribution networks. And the revolution that has begun in information pro-cessing, storage, and retrieval will cause many changes in communications within the business community.

A second trend likely to continue is increased automation. Machines take over the work of humans when it is economically sensible for them to do so. Automation increases the power of the individual to produce. The farmer can produce more corn, the miner more coal, and the assembly-line worker more automobiles. If we can solve the problems of technological unemploy-ment, automation can increase the standard of living and reduce work hours for everyone.

It is difficult to imagine total automation, where raw materials are fed in one end and finished products emerge from the other, yet many of our processes are approaching that point today. Totally automated factories in Germany, Japan, and the United States employ a capital-to-labor ratio pre-viously thought impossible. Warehouses are becoming automated to the point of eliminating everyone but a few clerical workers. Some flow processes in the petrochemical and pharmaceutical industries are nearing total automation.

As this trend continues, more employees in manufacturing will be technicians, managers, designers, and control specialists; semiskilled and unskilled workers will move into more labor-intensive service industries.

A third trend, the emphasis on the service industries, led us to become a "service economy" in the early 1970s, when people had the money and the leisure time to demand services. Firms specializing in fast foods, recreation, travel and tourism, and a multitude of personal services are increasing rapidly in absolute numbers, and the value of their output is growing as a percentage of the gross national product.

These new businesses provide a service rather than a product, but they still must convert inputs into outputs. They must make forecasts and purchase materials. Their activities must be planned, designed, scheduled, and controlled. It may be more difficult to deal with the quality of a service than a product, but it is no less important. As services continue to grow relative to products, the emphasis of POM will evolve into new applications of existing principles and techniques and the development of new techniques and methods of measurement and control.

A fourth trend representing a challenge for the future is production of goods and services on a worldwide scale. Many firms market their outputs in many countries, and, in some, the manufacturing process also transcends national boundaries. Cotton grown in the United States is processed into printed cloth and cut into patterns; the pieces then are shipped to the other side of the globe (Taiwan, Korea, or Hong Kong), where they are sewn into shirts; finally, the shirts are transported back to the United States to be sold. Some of our "American" cars are assembled in one European country from parts made in a half dozen other countries. In some cases, we have seen entire product lines (radios and black-and-white TVs, for example) migrate to other countries where wage rates, natural resources, or some other factors permit sufficient manufacturing economies to outweigh increased transportation costs.

The trend toward more international manufacturing will be enhanced by less expensive transportation methods and deterred by conflicts in international relations among governments. It is likely, however, that world trade will be much greater in the future. This will cause greater challenges for POM. When territorial boundaries are crossed, we also cross into different political and cultural ideologies. Our assumptions about the American worker and the methods we use to motivate and control his or her efforts may be inadequate unless we are able to adapt them to the new situations.

Functions of Production/Operations Management

The process of converting inputs into outputs requires certain functions to be performed. Some are design functions, which receive most attention when the business is formed and at periodic intervals when major changes are made. Others are control functions, which must be performed continuously if the organization is to operate successfully.

Design and Development of Products and Services

Business organizations, research laboratories, and independent inventors continuously are developing new products and services. Yet few products are truly "new." The Hula Hoop, so successful in the 1950s, was a plastic adaptation of the cane hoops used by children in the late nineteenth century. The Yo-Yo traces its history to ancient Egypt, although many refinements have since been made in materials and design. Most new products and services are variations and improvements on already existing products and services.

Innovations in complete detail, ready for manufacture, seldom spring into the mind of an inventor. Usually the germ of an idea is developed, refined, and tested over many months before a working prototype is produced. The original idea may be creative, but the development of that idea into a marketable product or service requires a systematic, scientific study involving diligent work and a penchant for detail. Product specifications must be developed to assure that the item can be produced at a reasonable cost and of a desired quality.

Most large organizations, and many small ones, have research and development departments that study new products and new processes for their manufacture. Few companies can afford to produce the same product in the same way, year after year; nor can they rely on copying the innovations of others.

In service industries, this function is not as well developed—but it should be. "Product specifications" is a common term, but "service specifications" sounds unfamiliar. Services also should be specified in advance in terms of level of service, line of services, hours of availability, and many other more detailed characteristics if the organization is to be competitive.

Facilities Location

The proper location for the organization's facilities can be a one-time decision when the business is formed, or it may be a frequently recurring problem. The location decision may be critical to some firms and inconsequential to others. For example, the management of a small firm that makes garden tools for a major retailer may have to decide only on the original location, which may be anywhere within a 50-mile radius of the customer. A large fast-food chain, however, may be opening a new outlet every week, and the specific location chosen may be the most critical factor in determining the success of each outlet.

The location decision must weigh and combine costs of land and building, tax rates, distribution availability, customer access, growth potential, competitors' locations, suppliers' locations, energy sources, community acceptance, and a host of other factors. Depending on the importance and frequency of the decision, decision-making methods can range from simple rules of thumb and judgment to complex computer algorithms.

Capital Equipment

Included in capital equipment are the functions of determining the capital equipment needed, acquiring it at a reasonable cost, installing it, providing for both routine maintenance and emergency repair, and eventually replacing it. As with the location decision, capital equipment decisions can be simple or complex. Large manufacturing firms succeed or fail on the basis of the management of their capital assets. Service firms often have minimal material inventories but huge investments in capital. One obvious example is a dentist's office, but airlines, trucking companies, and rental firms also fall into this category.

The small firm making only occasional capital acquisitions often can rely on the equipment supplier to provide much of the analysis. For example, a lumber yard needing a forklift can get need assessments and competitive bids from two suppliers and then simply pick the best deal.

Facilities Layout

The arrangement of the process within the physical facilities influences the efficiency of the firm. Layout for a manufacturing plant should follow a logical sequence so that materials can flow smoothly through the process with a minimum of handling. For service functions, such as those performed by a bank teller, equipment and materials should be arranged to provide easy access and minimal delay. Where several service functions interact, they should be arranged in sequence according to the mainstream of customer flow through the process.

Unfortunately, many manufacturing and service operations are not laid out efficiently. This may be because they were never carefully arranged, but it is more likely because the parameters have changed. New machines have been added, old ones replaced, different products now are being produced, or space originally designated for material storage has been converted to office space for clerical workers. Few layouts are perfect, yet it is difficult to determine when a layout is bad enough to justify the obvious costs of disrupting production to move equipment and rearrange facilities.

Work Design and Measurement

Individual tasks within the production process must be designed to achieve goals of efficiency and cost. The higher the volume, the more critical the design. When a few seconds of unnecessary activity are eliminated from routine, repetitive jobs with short cycle times, thousands of dollars can be saved.

Work design and measurement are necessary for manpower control. The price of the output is largely a function of the labor and material it contains.

If material usage, including scrap and waste, must be accurately measured and controlled, so, too, should the labor component. The problems associated with measuring labor efficiency are more difficult than with material, but they are not insurmountable.

Work design and measurement are not as widespread in services as in manufacturing, because services are less repetitive. Since services generally are more labor-intensive, however, the need for more accurate labor measurement and control is critical, and the potential payoff is great.

Production Forecasting

Forecasting is necessary if the business firm is to anticipate the demand for its products and services. Sufficient time must be allowed to acquire inputs and transform them into outputs at the time and place needed. Forecasts can be based on analysis of past data, consideration of current events, and/ or educated guesses about future developments.

Both simple and complex statistical techniques are available to help the decision maker form a reasonable and accurate prediction of needs. These forecasts then become the basis of the plans and schedules for buying, manufacturing, and other activities of the firm.

Production Planning and Scheduling

In order to coordinate the many diverse yet dependent operations of an organization, a master plan of activities and a schedule of their timing is needed. Each operating unit then should derive from the master plan the information necessary to coordinate the activities for which it is responsible. Careful planning anticipates the needs for people, materials, and equipment so that sufficient lead time is available to make changes where necessary.

Planning and scheduling are dynamic activities. No matter how carefully initial plans are formed, unanticipated events will occur, and rescheduling will be necessary. Some activities may need to be expedited; some may need to be delayed. The planners and schedulers of the firm perform a juggling act with resources and available time in attempting to best utilize the firm's capacity to produce.

Purchasing/Materials Management

All organizations use materials. The material input may account for as much as 80 percent of the value of the output or for as little as 1 percent. The effort devoted to purchasing and materials management should reflect this relative importance; most firms place too little, rather than too much, emphasis on this activity.

The purchasing function includes researching, analyzing, and selecting vendors. Negotiation of contracts or other buying agreements are made to assure that the firm obtains the right quality, at the right time, in the right quantity, in the right place, and at the right price. The purchasing manager is responsible for vast amounts of the company's money, and failure to achieve any of these objectives will result in a less profitable operation.

Inventory Management

Once material is obtained, it must be stored—before it is processed, at intermediate stages in the process, and at the end of the process. These inventories—known as raw materials, work in process, and finished goods— represent a sizable portion of the firm's assets. Adequately controlled, the firm can be efficient. Inadequately controlled, the firm loses money through excess storage and handling costs, obsolescence, pilferage, breakage, and the opportunity costs of having too much or too little inventory on hand.

The essence of the problem is finding the balance between too much and too little. Economic ordering and lot size formulas and techniques, as well as material requirements planning, aid the decision maker in achieving this balance.

Quality Control

Production planning and scheduling are responsible for the *quantity* and timing of production; quality control is responsible for its *quality*. No amount of inspection can make a bad product or service a good one. Quality must be designed and manufactured into the product. It is essential, however, that the company monitor the quality of incoming materials, goods in process, and finished items to assure that quality goals are being met or that necessary corrective action is taken.

A popular misconception is that quality should be maximized. Although customers may want higher quality, they may not be willing to pay the resulting price. The rational manager sets a quality standard that is acceptable to the customer and yet economically feasible to produce. Like other production decisions, it is a matter of finding a balance between too much and too little quality.

Quality is no less important to service industries, although it may be more difficult to define and measure. Many advances are being made, but much work remains to be done on the application of existing principles and the development of new techniques to control the quality of services.

The functional areas outlined in this section form a plan for the remainder of the book. Chapter 2 deals with product and service design and development. The related functions of work design and location and the layout of facilities and equipment are combined in chapter 3. Forecasting, planning, and scheduling for production are the subjects of chapter 4. Chapter 5 details the fundamental principles and techniques of purchasing and materials management. Inventory control is the subject of chapter 6. And controlling the quality of output is addressed in chapter 7.

Before exploring each of these areas, however, several basic concepts of POM should be understood. The first of these is a classification format for manufacturing firms.

Types of Manufacturing

Manufacturing firms could be classified according to size, type of product, location, or many other variables. A classification more useful to the study of POM concepts, however, is a subdivision based on the type of process employed.

Job Shop Production

Job shops do work in small lot sizes rather than manufacturing the same product continuously. In a print shop, for example, many different jobs go on at any one time. The press will be set up to run one job; when that is completed, the press will be set up to run the next job. In the meantime, the first job is routed to other areas, where it is folded, collated, stapled, trimmed, packaged, and shipped. Each work area in the job shop performs its function on each job as it arrives. When, for example, packaging jobs arrive in rapid succession from other work areas, a waiting line of jobs develops; at other times, when no jobs are ready to be packaged, the packaging facilities are idle. One of the major problems in a job shop is scheduling the work in the proper amount and sequence to balance the costs of idle time against the costs of having jobs waiting.

The resources in a job shop are general rather than specialized. Basic materials can be used in many different jobs with different specifications. Equipment should be adaptable to different uses. Similarly, the skills of the employees should be broad enough to allow them to work on any job within their area.

Repetitive Production

A second type of manufacturing is repetitive production, often associated with a moving assembly line. It involves high-volume production of discrete units such as automobiles, pencils, chairs, or bicycles. When the volume for one item is high enough, repetitive manufacture is more economical than the job-shop method. Specialized materials, equipment, and skills are employed to produce this one item and are not used on anything else.

The automobile industry is a good example of repetitive manufacturing. The lot size for a given model may be hundreds of thousands, and the production run will be almost one year. Specialized equipment is built to perform a task on this particular model, and workers are trained to be responsible for only one job. The critical problem in repetitive production is not daily scheduling but setting up and balancing the jobs so the process will run smoothly and efficiently.

Intermittent Production

Repetitive production and job-shop production are extremes; the intermediate level between the extremes is called intermittent production. Production runs are longer than in a job shop but not as long as in repetitive production. Equipment is set up to run a job for several weeks and then is changed for a run of another product. The degree of specialization of the materials, equipment, and skills falls between the needs of the other two methods. Toy manufacturers, food processors, and some clothing manufacturers are examples of intermittent production.

Flow Process Production

A fourth type of manufacturing is the flow process method, characterized by the continuous flow required by production technology. The petroleum industry, for example, does not produce discrete units; it transforms crude oil into various end products through a process that rarely stops. Individual operations do not exist; the input gradually is converted to outputs. Because of these special characteristics, a strong emphasis is placed on the design and planning aspects of the process. Once it begins, replanning is seldom possible, so the process is carefully monitored and controlled to meet the original plan.

Project Production

Project production, the fifth category of manufacturing, is employed when only one very complex unit is being produced. Examples include building construction, shipbuilding, and missile programs. Since there is only one unit but myriad interrelated activities, the functions of planning and scheduling, quality control, and other POM functions assume a different meaning. Special techniques, such as PERT and CPM (see chapter 4), apply directly to the unique requirements in this type of manufacturing.

Classification of Service Organizations

This classification scheme applies mainly to the production of goods; service firms do not fall into such clearly defined categories. In some service firms, such as restaurants, a physical product is a part of the output, and some aspects of this classification format apply. For example, fast-food chains resemble repetitive manufacturing, while a Japanese restaurant might be viewed as a job shop since meals are prepared individually at the table. Similarly, a wedding banquet for 250 people could be considered a project and employ many of the planning and scheduling techniques of project management.

Firms, whether manufacturing or service, are classified by process in order to group similar types of firms with similar problems. To the extent that a service firm approximates the characteristics and shares the problems of a given type of manufacturing firm, it probably can employ the problem-solving methodology already used in the other firms in that group. Inventing or reinventing problem-solving methods is a costly and often unnecessary activity.

Goals of Production/Operations Management

To remain economically viable, a firm must convert inputs into outputs effectively and efficiently. It must be concerned with both the unit cost of its products and services and their contribution to profit. In addition, the enlightened firm will look at various aspects of productivity and always seek improvement. Each of these overlapping goals will be defined and briefly discussed.

Effectiveness

Effectiveness is the degree to which the purpose of the organization is achieved. The purpose of a firm in the transportation industry is to move materials and/or people; the more it moves, the more effective it is. Effectiveness requires eliminating unnecessary activities and output that fail to meet the quality standard. It is a combination, therefore, of how much and how well the output of the firm conforms to the purpose of the organization. Effectiveness can be measured by sales, market share, consumer opinion, and other global measures, as well as by comparing specific results to specific company objectives.

Efficiency

Efficiency refers to how fast the output is produced and the relative amount of resources consumed. Efficiency generally relates to reducing waste—of time, effort, and/or materials. Greater efficiency can result through technical changes, such as better, faster machines; through managerial changes, such as better planning, scheduling, and control activities; or through behavioral changes in the workers, such as working smarter or working harder. Improved efficiency means greater output for a given amount of resources, which leads to greater benefits for all concerned.

Unit Cost

One of the best "how are we doing?" measures available to the production manager is unit cost. If the production manager is doing a good job of controlling the quantity, quality, and price of the inputs and is carefully planning, scheduling, and controlling the process, those efforts will be reflected in a favorable unit cost. One must be wary, however, for many different accounting methods exist to determine unit cost. In making comparisons between firms or divisions or from year to year, comparable accounting procedures should be used.

Contribution to Profit

Because profit is one of the major objectives of the firm, contributions to profit should be recognized. When comparing one product line with another or one division with another, measures of unit cost, efficiency, or effectiveness may not be meaningful. Contribution to profit—the excess of revenue over costs—can determine whether a product line should be expanded or discontinued. Contribution to profit also can be a factor in decisions regarding new capital equipment, plant location, research and development activities, and other areas where efficiency measures are incomplete or inappropriate.

Productivity

Perhaps the most often misunderstood objective is productivity. Productivity frequently is used to mean output per man-hour, but it really means any output-to-input ratio. The total productivity of the firm is the total of all outputs divided by the total of all inputs. This measure, however, seldom is found because of the difficulty of identifying and measuring all these factors in some common measurement unit. We usually deal with partial measures, such as labor productivity, capital productivity, or material productivity.

Productivity differs from efficiency in that efficiency seeks the maximum output from a *given* amount of resources. Productivity looks for the maximum *ratio* between the two and, thus, can involve a change in the output, the input, or both.

Productivity is critically important to individual business firms and to the economy as a whole. To remain profitable, a firm must maintain or improve its productivity. Improvements in a firm's productivity will lead to improved unit cost, profit, and return on investment. At the national level, improvements in productivity mean less inflation, better utilization of natural resources, and a stronger position in the world market.

Social Responsibility

Each of the other goals of POM should be pursued within a framework of socially responsible decisions and actions. Short-run cost reductions might be achieved by dumping pollutants into waterways, but the increased cleanup costs for society make this a bad decision. The firm should consider long-run as well as short-run costs and hidden costs as well as obvious costs.

Virtually every function within POM has social-responsibility implications. For example, the design of a product must consider safety features, such as avoiding the use of lead paint, even if they are not required by law. Scheduling decisions can enhance or disrupt the personal life of employees; quality-control decisions can affect the health and safety of customers.

Often the issues are difficult, and there may be no "correct answers." The economics of the situation may indicate that a plant should be closed or moved to another location, yet the effect on the local community could be devastating. Should the company operate the plant at a loss? The decisions on many such social-responsibility issues still are being debated.

Careers in Production/Operations Management

Positions in the production/operations area span the organization from the lowest to the highest levels. Many opportunities are available for the college graduate, and it is possible to spend an entire career in various areas of the production/operations function while progressing from an entry-level position to the ranks of upper management. Assignments in POM also provide a good background for entry into other areas of the organization.

The matrix in figure 1-2 indicates some of the common position titles at the entry, department-head, and division or corporate levels of the organization. This is but a small sample; a complete list would fill a book. One problem in compiling such a list is that different organizations use different terminology. In one company, for example, the title "planner" may refer to a very senior position, while in another firm, it may be an entry-level job.

In the area of forecasting, planning, and scheduling, a junior planner or scheduler could be responsible for compiling the machine, material, and work-force schedules for one or more of the manufacturing departments. The department manager is responsible for organizing all schedules and forecasts into a realistic master production schedule and then seeing that the plans are being carried out and taking corrective action where necessary. Although the department head is responsible for these activities, this position involves more supervision of the people performing the activities than actually doing the day-to-day work. At the corporate level, the vice president of planning will be concerned with a longer time span and more critical decisions, such as five-year forecasts, capacity additions, and major production changeovers.

Each of the other functions follows a similar pattern: entry-level jobs are more involved with *doing*, while upper-level jobs involve more supervision of the activities and long-range planning. Methods analysts redesign jobs, buyers

Level	Function						
	Forecasting, Planning, & Scheduling	Work Design, Location, & Layout	Purchasing	Inventory Control	Quality Control	Product Design & Development	Line
Division or Corporate	VP (or Director), Planning	VP, Plant Engineering	VP, Materials Management VP, Purchasing		VP, Product Quality	VP, R & D	VP, Manufacturing
Department	Manager, Production Control	Manager, Industrial Engineering	Purchasing Manager	Inventory Manager	Quality-Control Manager	Manager, Product Development	Department Manager
Entry Level	Scheduler/Planner	Methods Analyst	Buyer	Inventory Control Specialist	Inspector	Product Engineer	Supervisor or Management Trainee

Figure 1-2.   Career Tracks in POM

purchase materials, and inventory-control specialists make decisions about inventory levels, storage, and handling of materials.

Concern for professionalism within POM areas is reflected in the increased number of certification programs that have developed over the last decade. Spurred mainly by professional associations, these programs establish criteria for knowledge, skill, and experience required to carry out successfully the responsibilities of some POM jobs. Procedures then are developed to certify an individual as qualified; often the certification process requires individuals to pass a rigorous test and also may include education, experience, or other requirements. Although not required by law, certification can be a deciding factor for the firm when choosing from among candidates for a POM position.

Many certification programs are now in operation, and more are being planned. For example, the American Production and Inventory Control Society (APICS) conducts a series of tests leading to the designation "Certified in Production and Inventory Management" allowing Bill Jones to write his name as Mr. William Jones, CPIM. The National Association of Purchasing Management (NAPM) awards a C.P.M. (Certified Purchasing Manager) designation based on educational and experiential requirements and test results. Through the American Society for Quality Control (ASQC), an individual can earn a CQE (Certified Quality Engineer), CQT (Certified Quality Technician), or CRE (Certified Reliability Engineer).

While the certification programs promote professionalism in specialized POM functions, the performance of the functions at the entry level often requires a close relationship between managers and engineers or other specialists. In the government, for example, management analysts and industrial engineers work jointly on problems of layout, equipment selection, and job design. Under the supervision of the manager of industrial engineering, each contributes special expertise to the problem.

While it is possible to take a straight track to the top, advancing from inspector to manager of quality control to vice president of product quality, diagonal tracks involving lateral transfers also are common. Many firms prefer—and some insist—that a corporate-level director have some experience in each of the areas under his or her control. A vice president of materials management, therefore, could have started as a scheduler, then worked as a senior buyer, and progressed through other positions in several related areas.

One track deserves special mention. In virtually every business, whether manufacturing or service, there is a manufacturing or operations department. Beginning with the workers who create the product or service, the advancement track progresses through supervisor to department manager, plant manager, vice president of manufacturing, and president. These are the "line" positions, and in many organizations this is the shortest and surest route to the top. Automobile companies, for example, seldom have a top-level executive who has not had some line experience.

Service firms differ considerably from manufacturing firms (and from each other) in the way they organize these operations functions and the position titles they attach to them. These same functions must be performed, however, and the same general principles apply. An airline, for example, must carry an inventory of parts and supplies, and maintenance jobs must be carefully scheduled. Purchasing in a hospital obviously is a critical function; and, although job-design principles are being applied to health-care facilities, few have an industrial engineering department in their organization. Many POM positions in service industries are yet to be established, even though they are critically needed. Obviously, there is considerable opportunity for people to build new careers in many service organizations.

References

Adam, Everett, E., Jr., and Ebert, Ronald J. *Production and Operations Management.* 2nd ed. Englewood Cliffs, NJ: Prentice-Hall, 1982.

Chase, Richard B., and Aquilano, Nicholas J. *Production and Operations Management.* 4th ed. Homewood, IL: Richard D. Irwin, 1985.

George, Claude S., Jr. *The History of Management Thought.* 2nd ed. Englewood Cliffs, NJ: Prentice-Hall, 1972.

Hendrick, Thomas E., and Moore, Franklin G. *Production/Operations Management.* 9th ed. Homewood, IL: Richard D. Irwin, 1985.

Taylor, Frederick W. *The Principles of Scientific Management.* New York: Harper & Bros., 1911.

Discussion Questions

1. For each of the organizations listed below, (a) list the major inputs needed, (b) explain the nature of the conversion process, and (c) list the major outputs of goods and/or services.
   a. Boeing Aircraft
   b. American Airlines
   c. Bechtel Construction Company
   d. The Village Delicatessen
   e. Sears, Roebuck
   f. U.S. Bureau of Engraving and Printing

2. List and explain three examples of real companies for each category of manufacturing: project, job shop, intermittent, repetitive, and flow process. Give two examples of companies that contain two or more of these categories within the same firm.

3. Discuss possible classification systems for services—for example, services involving a product (restaurant) and those that do not (counseling) or those that require the customer's presence (barber shop) and those that do not (gardener).

4. Consider the ten functions of production management discussed in this chapter. Lay them out in time sequence; that is, which functions must be (can be) performed before another is begun?

5. Is it possible for a business firm to be effective but not efficient? Efficient but not effective? Effective and efficient but not productive? Discuss.

6. "Students are processed (educated) in 'batches' (classes). In that respect, a university is a giant job shop."
   a. Indicate whether you agree or disagree with this statement. In what respects is a university similar or dissimilar to a print shop? Consider, for example, the sequence of operations and the sequence of courses as well as the scheduling of jobs and the scheduling of classes.
   b. In a typical job shop, each job takes a different amount of time. Describe the scheduling problems that would result if every class were a different number of weeks in length.
   c. Is the registration procedure at your university more like one of the other forms of production? Which one?
   d. What would be necessary in order to educate students using a repetitive type of production? Describe the process.

7. Use the model presented in figure 1-1 to compare and contrast these two firms: a manufacturer of doghouses and a dog-grooming service.
   a. What are the major differences in the types and relative amounts of inputs needed?
   b. How do the conversion processes differ? Is the customer involved in the conversion process?
   c. Are there differences in the flows of funds and/or information from the environment to the firms? Explain.

8. Why is mass production only found in the twentieth century?

9. Most large banks have a facility called the operations center. What is the purpose of this facility and what work is performed there?

10. What is the purpose of a certification program such as CPIM or C.P.M.? What is the value to the person who is certified? How does this compare to licensing accountants, doctors, or lawyers?

Chapter 2

Design and Development of Products and Services

The basic purpose of any organization is either the making and selling of products or the rendering of certain services, or both. To remain in business, organizations must make sure that the design of the products they sell or the services they render are what the customers want and are willing to buy. Designing products and services that match customer needs is not an easy task. Not only are customer needs and preferences constantly changing but competition and advancing technologies also continually make current products and services obsolete. For example, not too many years ago the slide rule was a stable product in what appeared to be a mature and stable market. This market experienced radical changes, however, when technological advancements in the electronics industry prompted the introduction of the hand-held calculator. The electronic calculator quickly gained customer acceptance and rendered the slide rule obsolete. As a result, companies making slide rules either were forced out of business or had to design and develop new products that once again matched customer needs.

Products

A product is the tangible output of the production process. For example, in a washing-machine manufacturing plant, the inputs of sheet metal, electric motors, nuts, bolts, plastic agitators, and labor are converted by the production process (shaping and assembling) into finished products, which are completed washing machines. Products such as washing machines generally are brought into being because someone sees a customer need for an item that either no one is satisfying or that competitors are selling at too high a price. Clearly, if certain organizations in the past had not recognized specific customer needs and taken action to fulfull them, our society might be doing without many of the products, such as automobiles, television sets, telephones, and air conditioners, it now takes for granted.

Services

A service is something that satisfies a customer's need without providing a tangible, physical product. Examples of services include health care, education, transportation, garbage collection, and national defense. Services come into existence in much the same way as products: someone sees a customer need for a service that either no one is offering or that sells at too high a price. Today more than half the work force in the United States is engaged in rendering services rather than in producing products.

Product Life Cycle

With respect to the marketplace, most new products and services go through a product life cycle, the five stages of which are illustrated in figure 2-1.

1. Introduction Stage: Here the product is brand-new, high priced, and does not always work well. Furthermore, market awareness and acceptance of the product are minimal, with sales volume at a low level and growing very slowly. The only customers for the product at this point are the wealthy and the adventurous.

2. Growth Stage: The product now is accepted in the marketplace and making rapid sales gains as a result of the combined effects of promotion, distribution, improved dependability, standardization, increased use, and

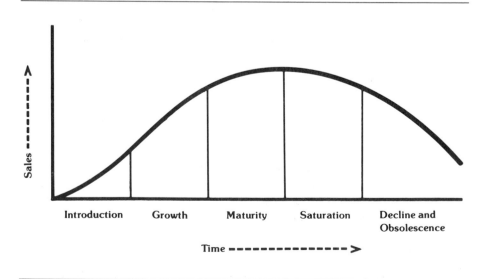

Figure 2-1.   Stages of the Product Life Cycle

lower selling prices. Customers buy the product with little prompting, but substantial profits gained by the innovating firm lure competition into the marketplace. The product begins to sell in much larger quantities as it becomes more commonly used.

3. Maturity Stage: Now a number of competitors have entered the market. The rate of sales growth begins to slow because of the declining numbers of people who still are unaware of the product. By now, the product has proved itself dependable in performance, and, because of increased competition, the product now is reasonably priced.

4. Saturation Stage: In this stage, nearly everyone who wants the product has bought it. Thus, sales level off at a rate determined by replacement demand plus sales resulting from population growth. Product promotion is very important in this stage, since the products of competitors differ very little, if at all. In our society, the markets for most automobiles, household appliances, and television sets have reached this stage.

5. Decline and Obsolescence Stage: Here, products are edged out of the market by better products or substitutes that are entering the growth and maturity stages of their life cycles. This does not happen to all products; for example, the scissors has been around for a long time, and newer products, such as the electric scissors, have not replaced it. On the other hand, the slide rule had been in the saturation stage for a long time before it was driven from existence by the electronic calculator.

Because most products go completely through the product life cycle and thus become obsolete, companies continually must work at designing and developing new products to take their place. Some of the specific activities involved in the design and development of these new products will be covered in the following sections of this chapter.

Research and Development

Research and development (R & D) refers to those activities principally concerned with investigation leading to the discovery of new scientific knowledge (research) and the translation of this new knowledge into marketable goods and services (development). If research had not produced the needed scientific knowledge, the development of television, jet airplanes, laser beams, computers, and many other products and services we take for granted today would not have been possible.

Product Policy

If a company is to yield maximum results from its R & D work, these efforts should take place within a well-defined product policy. Basically, product policy is a company's answer to "What kind of business are we in?" or "What is the basic purpose of our existence?'' For example, if a company's product policy stated that the basic business of the company was to produce oil, then its researchers would not direct their efforts toward harnessing solar or nuclear energy. Rather, these researchers should direct their efforts toward discovering more efficient ways to extract oil from coal shale or devising new techniques for finding off-shore oil deposits. On the other hand, if a company's product policy stated that the basic mission was to produce energy, then research efforts directed at harnessing solar or nuclear energy—or any energy form, for that matter—are well within the company's mission.

Without a well-defined product policy, a company will find that its R & D efforts lack a sense of direction and focus. It runs the risk of thinly spreading its R & D efforts over a multitude of areas rather than specifically pursuing those that have the greatest potential for strengthening the company's product line and thereby improving its competitive position. Unless a company can define its reason for being in terms of a specific product policy, it will not achieve the maximum return from its R & D efforts, and less relevant knowledge will be available from which to develop new marketable products and services.

Research and Development Applications

The basic purpose of research and development is the discovery of new knowledge that can be translated into marketable products and services. Within any business, there are a number of ways to apply R & D efforts.

New products. New products usually are brought into existence for one of three basic reasons:

1. To fill a gap in an existing product line: For example, a home-appliance producer may decide to manufacture a home air conditioner to make its line of home appliances more complete.

2. To supplement an already complete product line: For example, a house-paint manufacturer may decide to produce paint brushes to supplement an already complete line of home paints.

3. To capitalize on a potential market opportunity not related to existing product lines: For example, a full-line manufacturer of plastic toys may see a potentially strong market for plastic stocks for military rifles. This reason for introducing new products carries the most risk, since the company may be getting involved with markets and production processes about which it knows very little. Additional skills in product design, development, production, and marketing may be required to make the product successful.

One method of entering new product areas is to undertake a full-blown R & D effort of gathering new knowledge and translating this knowledge into the desired products. Although this type of effort has resulted in the manufacture of products such as the polio vaccine, television, and the jet engine, its high cost and associated risks normally limit such activity to the larger firms. On the other hand, the payoff to the firm making such a breakthrough via its own R & D efforts can be impressive.

Another way a firm can enter a new product area is to buy the R & D efforts of other firms. This often is done by marketing finished products under the buying company's own label. For example, a manufacturer and marketer of drafting supplies, such as rulers, triangles, and templates, may round out its product line by purchasing mechanical drawing instruments (which it does not produce) from a manufacturer in Germany and marketing them under its own label. The private product lines or brands of most large retailers are good examples of this practice. Although this practice tends to minimize R & D costs and risks, it also reduces the possibility of the substantial profits that often result from breakthroughs due to internal R & D activities.

Still another way a firm can enter a new product area is to merge with a firm that already has product lines in that area. The acquired firm has the skills necessary to produce and market the new product or product line. Mergers, however, do not always produce the anticipated results. Often a merger will cause new and unforeseen organizational problems that will adversely affect the new company's operations.

Modification of existing products.   One reason for modifying an existing product is to improve its customer appeal. This can be accomplished by: (1) reshaping the product to conform to current styling trends; (2) adding new features that will set the product uniquely apart, as was the intent when the remote-control channel selector was added to the color television product package; or (3) giving the product a new package that will produce a new look or image.

Another reason for modifying an existing product is to reduce its production costs. One of the best ways to reduce production costs is to redesign the product so that the cost of its materials is reduced. For example, a product often can be modified, without changing its functional performance, so that its production will require either less material, less expensive material (such as the substitution of plastic for metal), or both. Furthermore, material costs and assembly costs often can be greatly reduced if the product is modified to include the use of standard parts and components.

New uses for existing products.   Exploration of new uses for an existing product is often another objective of a firm's R & D efforts. R & D efforts are aimed at discovering ways that an existing product, or a slightly modified version of it, can be adapted to new markets. For example, a manufacturer of an industrial-grade liquid floor cleaner might take this same cleaner, dilute it, and market it as a liquid floor cleaner for households. This type of R & D activity, then, allows a firm to satisfy a greater number of customers within the realm of its existing products.

New packaging. Changing the packaging of an existing product involves changes in the size, shape, layout, or other external characteristics without affecting the product's purpose. Packaging changes often have the effect of creating a "new" product by giving regular customers, or customers in new markets, the existing product in a new form or in a quantity that is more satisfactory. For example, packaging frozen vegetables in one-pound packages instead of ten-ounce packages greatly improved sales to large-family consumers; the ten-ounce package contained too little product for such families, but two such packages contained too much.

By offering *eye-appealing* packages, a firm often can compete more effectively. A better box, wrapper, label, can, or bottle even may enable a relatively small and unknown firm to market successfully against established competitors.

Creating a physical model. The immediate outcome of an R & D effort is the creation of a physical model or prototype of the product. One reason for creating this model is to demonstrate that the ideas upon which the product is based are feasible. A second reason is to help management visualize how the product will look. Although these initial models may bear little physical resemblance to the final product, having such a model to evaluate facilitates design and development decisions regarding the final product. Before a decision can be made about a product's final specifications, however, much additional information from a number of sources will be required. The types of information still required, as well as some of the sources of this information, are discussed in the following section.

Product Design

Taking a physical model and modifying its design into a product that can be produced and marketed profitably requires information inputs from a number of areas within the firm as well as from the marketplace. Factors such as alternate material costs, use of standard parts and components, results of product tests, as well as inputs from market research, all must be considered. Once this needed information is gathered and properly analyzed, the specifications of the final product can be determined.

Material

Often the product designer can choose from among several different materials. For example, automobile hoods can be made out of aluminum, steel, or fiberglass. In choosing from among available material alternatives, the designer must consider: (1) the performance requirements of the product, (2) the relative costs of the alternate materials, (3) the relative processing costs associated with the alternate materials, (4) the effect of each material on the appearance of the final product, and (5) the relative availability of each material.

When two or more of the alternatives can produce the required performance, the lowest-priced alternative does not automatically win out. It may be that the highest-priced material costs less to process. Thus, the highest-priced alternative may be the most desirable alternative when *total* production costs are considered. For example, aircraft producers save a substantial sum of money by using higher-priced bronze rather than steel extrusions in aircraft elevator and rudder counterweights. Even though bronze is higher priced than steel, the savings in machining time more than offsets the increase in material costs.

A material alternative also may be desirable from the standpoint of performance, cost, and appearance but may be obtainable from only one supplier. In this case, a material decision is also a supplier decision, and the firm should carefully evaluate the reliability of the supplier's ability to meet desired future quantity requirements and delivery schedules. At a minimum, this decision calls for a thorough investigation of the supplier's available plant capacity, financial strength, and labor situation.

Value Analysis/Value Engineering

Value analysis/value engineering involves an organized, systematic study of every element of cost in a part, material, product, or service to ensure that it fulfills its function at the lowest total cost. VA/VE is the study of function and value. Function refers to the job that the material, part, product, or service performs. For example, the function of a ball-point pen may be "to write." Value is defined as the lowest end cost at which the function may be accomplished at the time and place required and with the quality required. For example, if the only function of a ball-point pen were to write, the least expensive pen probably would do the job. If, on the other hand, the pen must fulfill an additional function, such as indicating status, then perhaps a more expensive gold-filled pen would be required.

Although it may sound quite technical, VA/VE actually is a straightforward and basic approach designed to reduce material and production costs while ensuring that the product still fulfills its intended function in a satisfactory manner. A VA/VE study cannot be carried out effectively unless the function of the product is first determined—that is, "to write" or "to connote status," or both. Once the function of the product has been determined, the remainder of the study involves asking and objectively answering a number of basic questions about the particular item. Most companies develop a checklist to systematize this activity. In some cases, these checklists consist of hundreds of questions, such as:

1. Would a less costly design work as well?
2. Can a standard item be used?
3. Can the product's weight be reduced?
4. Can a less expensive material do the job?
5. Can the costs of packaging be reduced?
6. Does the item have a greater capacity than required?

By thoughtfully answering such questions, analysts generally will arrive at alternatives. If the answer to a particular question is not entirely satisfactory, this becomes the starting point for a more detailed investigation. The use of a well-developed checklist of questions focuses attention on those factors that may further reduce production costs.

The cost savings attributed to VA/VE efforts have been impressive. For example, one firm that had been using a specially designed screw costing 15¢ each found a way to make the screw for 1.5¢, resulting in an annual savings of $20,000. In another instance, a gasket costing $4.15 each when made in-house was found to cost 15¢ when purchased from an outside supplier.

Standardization

Standardization is the process of establishing agreement upon uniform identifications for certain characteristics of quality, design, performance, quantity, and service. A uniform identification that generally is agreed upon is called a *standard*. For example, if a person in the United States buys an electric appliance such as a toaster, the buyer knows that this toaster will operate on the same voltage available from the electrical outlets at home. Why? Because in the United States the voltage in homes has been standardized at 110 volts. Likewise, when you buy a light bulb, you know the bulb will screw into the available sockets at home because light bulb sockets in the United States are standard. Just think of the problems that would exist if each typewriter manufacturer's typewriter keyboard were arranged in a different configuration!

Standards, however, do not exist only for consumer products. They also exist for a wide variety of items used in manufacturing, such as nuts, bolts, screws, and electric motors. Without these standards, there could be no assembly line, since there would not be interchangeable parts. The lack of standards also would complicate repair services greatly. Many of the items we use on a daily basis would cost more to buy and maintain.

There are several reasons for incorporating, whenever possible, standard parts and components into the design of a product. The use of standard items in a company's products permits the company, as a whole, to purchase fewer items in larger quantities at lower prices. If fewer items are purchased, then fewer items need to be processed and stocked. This has the immediate effect of lowering purchasing, receiving, inspection, and accounts-payable costs. In addition, stocking fewer items makes controlling inventories and production easier and less costly, and it greatly simplifies assembly operations. Furthermore, since suppliers generally stock standard items in their inventories, deliveries can be made more quickly, allowing the firm to maintain lower inventory levels, which, in turn, result in another substantial saving. Thus, lower prices, lower processing costs, lower inventory costs, and lower scheduling costs all are reasons why a firm uses standard parts and components in the design of its products. As a result, a product can be brought to market at a lower total cost.

Modular Design

Modular design refers to designing products with easily detachable sections or modules. When an item fails, the whole module (of which the item is a part) is removed and replaced with a new module. The module that has failed either can be repaired at a central facility (which is usually less costly than on-site repair) or it can be discarded. For example, if a transistor in a television set fails, the whole printed circuit board (of which the transistor is a part) is removed and replaced.

The basic reason why industries, such as electronics, have turned to modular design has been the high cost of repair labor, which has made breakdowns associated with conventional forms of design extremely expensive. Under the modular design concept, the on-site time it takes to repair a complicated piece of electronic equipment is greatly reduced. If the replaced module is worth repairing, the repair work then can be accomplished at a central facility utilizing less expensive labor.

Modular design also is gaining rapid acceptance in the home-building industry. In this case, the impetus behind modular design is the high cost of construction labor. Under the modular design concept, standard house components (such as the bathroom) can be mass produced at a central facility with less expensive assembly labor. The components then are transported to the building site and put together utilizing only a fraction of the time and expensive labor associated with conventional construction methods.

Computer-aided Design (CAD)

Computer-aided design (CAD) is a complex and imaginative new tool that is revolutionizing the product design activity. CAD first was used in the aerospace industry and soon was adopted by the automobile industry to help deal with the horrendous engineering and design nightmare of downsizing the entire fleet of America's gas-guzzling cars. Today, because of the declining prices of computer equipment and the increased capabilities of computer software, CAD techniques commonly are used in many other industries as well.

Basically, CAD consists of a computer drawing pictures, on a television screen or cathode ray tube (CRT), of what the engineer has designed. The sophisticated CAD software is able to draw lines between points, creating a three-dimensional drawing that can be rotated to show all sides of the design. As a result, CAD greatly speeds up the normally slow and laborious work of drafting.

CAD is an especially effective way to design and analyze products because the computer communicates with the designer directly in pictures. By looking at these pictures, the designer is able to absorb and interpret the informational content of the design much faster than if he or she were looking at an array of numbers or words and then trying to translate them into mental pictures. Furthermore, if the necessary programming has been done, the designer can analyze and test the things designed by subjecting them to electronically simulated temperature changes, mechanical stresses, or other potential problems the product is likely to encounter in its real-world application. For example, color graphics can be used to show heat or stress points of a design in red and cool points in blue, thus enabling the engineer to understand more easily the design's temperature fields.

Such on-screen testing and analysis can save huge amounts of time and money associated with the more traditional way of designing a product— that is, building a prototype, testing it, modifying the design, and then retesting the prototype. Products designed using a CAD system are more likely to work properly when built, since many of the problems associated with a new or modified product can be removed before the product leaves the design stage.

Market Research Inputs

Thus far, all the inputs to the product design process have come from within the firm. But because the success of a product ultimately is determined by the consumer, he or she also should be allowed to express opinions about the product's design. This important information is gathered through market research.

In the initial stage of a product's development, market information concerning the product's salability normally is gathered by using a survey questionnaire. The questionnaire is simply a list of carefully phrased questions to be used either to guide a series of personal interviews with potential customers or to elicit desired information in a selected mailing to potential customers.

Information collected should indicate the size (quantity) of a potential market over time for alternative product characteristics (designs, packages, quality, and reliability levels, as well as any other selected operating features) and alternate prices. The survey also should provide valuable information concerning the activities of major competitors, styling trends, and predictable seasonal variations in sales, if they exist.

Information gathered this way can be extremely useful in guiding a product through its final design and development stages. Without such information, it would be difficult to differentiate between products that only seem to be a good idea from those with sound market potential. For example, consider the individual who decided he had the greatest idea in the world for packaging and marketing unprocessed wheat bran. He packaged his product in a rustic brown paper bag with an eye-catching sea-gull logo printed on the front. A recipe incorporating bran was printed on the back of the bag, and a copy of a copyrighted bran recipe was included inside. Our entrepreneur also decided to price his product far below his competitors in order to gain immediate market acceptance. The whole idea seemed so good that the fellow proceeded, without conducting even the most basic market research, to buy 20,000 printed bags, enough bran to fill them, and enough master cartons to ship them. The initial investment was $10,000.

When sales did not pick up as rapidly as expected—in fact, they never even got off the ground—the bran man decided to conduct a survey to find the problem. The results indicated that the bag idea, although quaint and seemingly clever, was unattractive to retailers because the bags couldn't be stacked on the shelf the way conventional cereal boxes could. Furthermore, since unprocessed bran was a slow-moving item regardless of its price, most retailers were reluctant to give the product any shelf space to start with. To make matters even worse, the master cartons were the wrong size; when the allocated shelf space was completely filled, there still were some bags of bran left in the carton, which then had to be put in inventory in the storeroom. Conclusion: the idea was a loser to start with. Cost of the market survey: less than $100. Had this individual conducted the survey *before* taking action, he would have saved himself $9,900 and a lot of grief.

Resources

The resources of a firm, including its facilities and equipment, the skills of its personnel, and its financial strength, have an important impact on the final design of each product that will be manufactured. The closer the production requirements of a product match the capabilities of a firm's existing equipment and personnel resources, the more efficient will be the manufacturing process. On the other hand, the less the production requirements of a product match the firm's resources, the less efficient the product will be to manufacture. For example, if a firm currently produces products on an assembly line, it probably would not be in the company's best interest to initiate a new product requiring much custom work at individual work stations. Such a move probably would be inefficient because the workers would have to learn new skills, new equipment would have to be purchased, material handling patterns would have to be altered, and inventories would have to be adjusted.

The design of a product should not be approved nor the decision made to produce it until the firm objectively examines its financial condition to ensure that it has the necessary dollar resources to see the product through to the point where it begins to return a profit. For a major new product (especially one requiring substantial investments in new equipment and facilities), this often takes a long time, since buildings may have to be built, equipment purchased and installed, and raw materials and parts purchased. In addition, the actual production of a brand-new product initially proceeds slowly since it usually takes time to work the "bugs" out of a new production system. Each of these activities takes time and is costly. But no money is coming in from the new product's sales to help offset these costs. To make matters worse, when the product finally does hit the marketplace, initial sales normally are slow until market acceptance for the product is gained. Thus, if a firm doesn't have the financial resources (cash or credit) to offset these initial costs, the company may go out of business before the product ever has a chance to realize its long-term potential.

Testing

Before a product is placed into production, prototypes of the product should be tested sufficiently to ensure that the final product will perform its intended function. This is the stage of product design where steel-belted tires are run over boards full of nails and where wrist watches are thrown into cement mixers or worn by football players during practice. The main concerns here are quality and reliability as they relate to the product's intended function.

Another important factor in product testing is consumer safety. Recalls of products are expensive, both in terms of the cost of the recall and the damaging effect on a company's image. A good example is the product-recall problem Firestone Tire and Rubber Company faced with certain models of its steel-belted radial tires. One major goal of product testing should be to preclude such product-use problems and recalls.

Pilot-production Run

After all the inputs concerning materials, value analysis/value engineering, standardization, market research, company resources, and product testing have been incorporated into the product's design, a complete set of tentative specifications is drafted, and the product is put through a pilot-production run. A pilot-production run involves the manufacture of a small quantity of a new product under simulated normal production conditions. The purpose is to "shake down," or test, the new product as well as the new system and to remove any product defects or process inefficiencies that still may exist. Once this stage is completed, the product design becomes definite, and the product's specifications can be finalized.

Product Description

After a product design is established, much supporting work must be done before finished products begin to roll off the end of the production line. Materials of the right quality and quantity must be purchased for delivery at a time specified by the firm's production schedule. Once the required materials are delivered, certain operations, such as cutting, drilling, and machining, may have to be performed. Finally, these materials must be assembled in a certain order if the final product is to perform correctly. None of these activities could begin to occur with any degree of efficiency without the entire product being completely, clearly, and accurately described to those individuals who are required to take action.

Specifications

Product specifications refer to the detailed description of a product. This description usually includes a list of the product's measurable characteristics (dimensions, weights, volumes, and tolerances), the different parts and components that go into the product, and a detailed set of directions stating how the product is to be assembled. For a complicated product such as an aircraft, the specifications consist of thousands of pages of detailed descriptions and blueprints showing every part, dimension, material, and method of assembly. Since an aircraft is so complicated, large teams of experts must develop adequate specifications.

The more simple the product, the simpler its specifications. This should be but is not always the case, however. For example, the U.S. government specification for a mousetrap contains more than 120,000 words plus pages of supporting literature!

Bill of Materials

In addition to clear, complete, and accurate product specifications, additional descriptive documentation is necessary to manufacture a product efficiently. The bill of materials (B/M), usually developed by the design engineer from the product's specifications, lists all the items, including the quantities of each, required to produce one unit of finished product. For example, the B/M for a bicycle would specify that two pedals, two handle grips, and one seat (among other things) are required to produce one finished bicycle. An example of a B/M for the manufacture of a Yo-Yo is illustrated in figure 2-2.

An important function of the bill of materials is that it, along with a production schedule, can be sent directly to the purchasing department to communicate the production department's exact need for materials. The total amount of each part required for production then can be determined by multiplying the quantity shown on the B/M by the quantity scheduled into production. For example, if the production schedule calls for 2,000 Yo-Yos during the next month, multiplying this final output by the quantities shown in figure 2-2 tells purchasing that 4,000 wooden discs, 2,000 connecting pins, 2,000 strings, 80 ounces of glue, 200 ounces of paint, and 2,000 cardboard boxes will be required.

After computing the total number of each item required for production, purchasing then can check the firm's inventory to see if any of the parts currently are in stock. Purchasing then will buy those materials needed to complete the production schedule. For example, if 4,000 wooden discs are required for production and 2,000 of the discs are in stock, then purchasing needs to buy only 2,000 additional discs to fulfill the requirement.

Product Description Yo-Yo		
Part or Material Number	Part Description	Quantity per Assembly
2010	Wooden Disc	2
2011	Connecting Pin	1
2012	3 Feet of String	1
2013	Glue	.04 oz
2014	Paint	.1 oz
2015	Cardboard Box	1

Figure 2-2.   Bill of Materials for a Yo-Yo

Route Sheet

The route sheet lists the sequence of production operations necessary to make the finished product. This will include inspection as well as assembly operations. The route sheet contains a separate entry for each operation performed on a different machine or in a different labor center. As an aid in production planning and scheduling, the route sheet almost always includes the standard times (when available) allowed for setting up each operation and producing each piece after the setup has been approved. An example of the route sheet for the production of a Yo-Yo is shown in figure 2-3.

Designing Services

Services satisfy customers' needs without providing a tangible product or item. Examples of service organizations include hospitals, schools, airlines, refuse collectors, fire departments, and government at all levels. The service sector has been growing at a faster rate than other sectors of the economy, and today more than half the people working in the United States are producing services rather than products.

Product Description Yo-Yo

Operation Number	Dept. Number	Machine Number	Operation Description	Setup Time (Minutes)	Per Piece Time (Minutes)
1	13	383	Paint wooden discs	1.3	.015
2	8	211	Connect discs with connecting pin	.75	.02
3	6	101	Attach string	.5	.01
4	7		Inspect		
5	21	622	Package	1.0	.015

Figure 2-3.   Route Sheet for a Yo-Yo

Types of Services Offered

Designing and developing a service involves the same type of analysis as conducted by a manufacturer considering a new addition to its product line. The organization's goals, facilities, equipment, personnel, and financial strength all must be analyzed and considered, along with the needs, desires, and willingness to pay of potential consumers. As a result of such analyses, some colleges and universities have decided to offer a wide array of courses, while others have chosen to offer fewer, more specialized courses. Similarly, certain insurance agencies sell only life insurance, whereas others offer property and casualty insurance, along with investment opportunities in mutual funds.

Governmental units at all levels also must decide what services to offer their citizens. For example, should the federal government provide employment opportunities in high labor-surplus areas? Should state governments provide low-cost rapid transit in their metropolitan areas? Should city governments provide health services, day-care centers, and job-training programs?

After a service organization determines the array of service its consumers want, it then must examine its resources to determine what it can offer. Only a very few service organizations have the necessary resources to offer all the services they deem worthwhile. For many tax-supported organizations, a developing problem has been that the cost of providing many services has increased at a faster rate than tax income. As a result, many state, county, and city governments have been forced to make some difficult choices concerning which services they will continue to offer and which will be discontinued. For example, the passage of Proposition 13 in California forced the elimination of many summer education programs and the scaling down of summer recreation programs, resulting in the layoff of thousands of employees.

Level of Service

The level of services offered refers not only to the types of services offered but also the availability of these services to the customers. Issues here include where to locate service facilities and when to make these services available to customers. Resolving these issues involves a balancing, on the part of the organization, of its capability in offering the services its customers want against the need to operate economically. For example, until fairly recently nearly all banks were located in a downtown area in a single central facility. They were open only five days a week for a limited period of time, referred to as "bankers' hours." Today, many banks have found it more profitable to serve their customers by scattering a number of branches throughout the area they serve In addition, many banks now keep some of their branches open in the evenings and on Saturdays while also providing limited services, such as a mechanical teller that is available 24 hours a day seven days a week.

Service as Part of the Product Package

When a company markets a product, it usually provides more than just a physical entity with its associated aesthetic and functional features. Instead, it sells an entire "product package," which includes accessories, installation, instruction on use, and the assurance that service facilities will be available to meet the customer's needs after the sale. Providing satisfactory customer service can be the most important competitive edge a company has. Very often, if satisfactory service is not part of the product package, many potential customers will not be interested in the product, and present customers even may switch to a competing product. For example, when a customer firm decides which manufacturer's copy machine to buy or lease, it considers carefully the level of service accompanying the product. Furthermore, when a company currently using a copy machine decides to change brands, the reason most frequently cited is "poor service."

Developing Specifications for a Service

Service specifications refer to the detailed description of a service to be performed. This description normally includes a list of the resources (materials, equipment, and labor) needed to perform the service, a detailed set of directions for delivering the service, and a list of measurable characteristics (criteria for evaluating acceptable and unacceptable performance) associated with satisfactory performance. Generally, the more complicated and involved the service to be performed, the more extensive the specifications. For example, the specifications for maintaining and operating all aspects of Glacier National Park on behalf of the federal government are quite extensive indeed. On the other hand, the specifications relating to cleaning a square yard of a particular grade of carpeting are straightforward and brief.

Specifications for services are every bit as important as they are for products. Having such service specifications greatly enhances the relationship between the provider of the service and potential customers. When such specifications are available, conflicts resulting from a difference between what the customer expected to obtain and what the service business expected to provide are reduced.

Developing a Bill of Materials for a Service

The bill of materials (B/M) for a service usually contains a list of all the materials and activities, including the quantity of each required to produce one unit of a completed service. Although the concept of "units of completed service" at first may appear somewhat nebulous, this really is not the case. For example, the unit of completed service for having some carpet cleaned would be "a square yard." The unit of measure for having a roof shingled is stated in terms of "100 square feet" increments, while the unit of completed service for a car wash would be stated either in terms of time (i.e., for each five minutes, the user must deposit another quarter) or in terms of the number of cars completed.

It is important that some unit of completed service be agreed upon and a bill of materials be developed if a service organization expects to compete over the long run. For example, a car wash owner/manager must know precisely how much soap, water, white-wall tire cleaner and hot wax it takes to wash one car satisfactorily. If this information were not known, there would be no way for the owner/manager to price the service intelligently. The owner/manager might price the service very competitively and attract droves of customers, only to find out later that he had failed to cover all costs and must, therefore, go out of business. This type of miscalculation is all too common among small service-oriented organizations.

An example of a B/M for a car wash is illustrated in figure 2-4. If, for example, the owner of the car wash forecasted that he would be washing 500 cars per week, he could determine how much material would be required simply by multiplying 500 times the amounts shown in figure 2-4. If this were the case, the owner would need to provide 1,500 ounces of detergent, 250 ounces of white-wall cleaner (assuming half the cars to be washed had white-wall tires), 6,000 gallons of water, and 2,000 ounces of hot wax.

Product Description

Car Wash

Material Number	Material Description	Quantity Per Unit (Washing One Car)
3010	Detergent	3 oz.
3011	White-wall Cleaner	1 oz.
3012	Water	12 gals.
3013	Hot Wax	4 oz.

Figure 2-4.   Bill of Materials for a Car Wash

References

Groover, J. D., and Zimmers, E. W., Jr. *CAD/CAM: Computer Aided Design and Manufacturing*. Englewood Cliffs, NJ: Prentice-Hall, 1984.

Hayes, R. H., and Wheelwright, S. "The Dynamics of Process-Product Life Cycles." *Harvard Business Review*. 59 (March-April 1979): 127-36.

Hayes, R. H., and Wheelwright, S. *Restoring Our Competitive Edge: Competing Through Manufacturing*. New York: John Wiley & Sons, 1984.

Hegland, Donald E. "CAD/CAM Integration—Key to the Automatic Factory." *Production Engineering*. 28 (August 1981): 31-35.

Moore, Franklin G., and Hendrick, Thomas E. *Production/Operations Management*. 8th ed. Homewood, IL: Richard D. Irwin, 1985.

Discussion Questions

1. Discuss the importance of the product life cycle as it relates to new-product design and development.

2. What are the basic differences between products and services?

3. What is a product policy, and how can it help make R & D efforts more efficient?

4. Discuss the concept of standardization and how it can help reduce production costs.

5. Discuss the interrelationship of specifications, the bill of materials, and the route sheet for a specific product.

6. What are the similarities between the specifications and bill of materials for a product and the specifications and bill of materials for a service?

Chapter 3

Location, Layout, Work Study, and Job Design

In designing the operating system of an organization, four factors must be considered to develop and sustain a competitive and profitable operation. They are:

1. Location—the regional, community, and site factors involved in determining either an original, replacement, or additional location of manufacturing, warehousing, office, or service facilities;

2. Layout—the arrangement of machines, equipment, materials handling, aisles, service areas, storage areas, and work stations within the facility;

3. Work study—the design of work procedures and methods, coupled with a work-measurement system, that facilitates usable work standards for planning and controlling operations; and

4. Job design—the arrangement of the work activities of an individual or group to best meet the requirements of the organization, the technology, and the worker.

Facilities Location

Improper location usually results in increased production and distribution costs, placing an otherwise efficiently managed company at a competitive disadvantage. The location decision takes on added significance because that choice, once made and implemented, cannot be changed without considerable financial loss. Therefore, serious attention should be devoted to the location problem from the very beginning.

Sequence of Location Choices

The facilities location decision involves three phases: (1) the region or general area, (2) the particular community within the region selected, and (3) the specific site within the community.

Regional factors requiring serious consideration include:

1. Closeness to markets. Distance increases transit time and costs and thereby affects the service provided.

2. Access to materials and vendors. This determines transport times and costs for materials, supplies, tools, equipment, and components supplied by vendors.

3. Transportation and communication facilities. Prompt, regular, dependable, and low-cost shipment and communication services are essential. Depending upon the volume, frequency, and cost of movements, the company may prefer rail, truck, air, or barge carriers—or some combination of these.

4. Concentration of skilled labor and the overall labor supply. The objective is to develop and maintain an effective work force with minimum recruiting and training costs. Favorable regional wage rate differentials are a strong plus factor in situations where labor cost represents a major part of a firm's total operating cost.

5. Climate. Climate may be a major factor in attracting the desired labor supply. A mild climate generally is preferable; its influence is evident in the rapid growth of the Sunbelt states in both manufacturing industries and population.

Factors that affect the location decision at the community level include the following:

1. Labor supply. This should be sufficient to provide the number of people and skills to be employed in both new and existing facilities.

2. Managerial preferences. Many plants are located in the community where the founder lived when the firm was established.

3. Community facilities and living conditions. Schools, churches, medical facilities, shopping facilities, recreational and cultural opportunities, available housing, and municipal services (such as water, power, sewer, garbage, and police and fire protection) are important in recruiting an adequate work force.

4. Laws and taxes. These may restrict or support a firm's operation.

5. Availability of suitable sites. The desirable locations already may be occupied.

6. Attitudes. The community, labor groups, and other business firms may have coop͏ ͏ive attitudes or be resistant to any change.

7. Inducements. The community may make financial and/or tax inducements to attract the organization.

The following specific site location factors within a community should be considered.

1. Size must be adequate for present needs and sufficient for future expansion.

2. Topography, drainage, and soil conditions of the plot should be suitable and permit reasonable construction costs.

3. Land costs, plus total development costs, should be realistic.

4. Utilities, such as electricity, gas, water, and sewers, should be available on a dependable basis at a reasonable cost.

5. Transportation facilities, such as roads, rail sidings, and airports, should facilitate the efficient and low-cost receipt and distribution of the materials and the necessary travel of key personnel.

6. Provision for waste disposal and environmental considerations should minimize restrictive legislation, control costs, and prevent loss of public support.

City Versus Rural Location

Arguments exist on both sides of the city versus rural or small-town location controversy. Sites for city locations are more limited in number and size and have higher purchase costs and, normally, higher taxes. Conversely, rural sites are less expensive and more available and have fewer legal restrictions and lower taxes. Cities frequently have better public transportation but more traffic congestion and poor parking facilities. The city labor supply normally is larger and more skilled but is more likely to be unionized. Cities normally provide better educational and recreational facilities, more service industries and professional organizations, and a larger vendor base.

Suburban locations have most of the advantages of both the city and the rural location, with few disadvantages of either. Consequently, many firms today compromise in favor of a suburban location.

Relocation

Relocation may be required for such reasons as product diversification, company expansion through vertical integration, rising sales or shifting markets, depletion of material resources, obsolescence of plant facilities and equipment, and geographic dispersion for better flow of materials and products.

When confronted with a need to expand, a firm has several alternatives:

1. Expand in the present location.

2. Remain static and let the competition get the new business.

3. Maintain existing size, but use subcontractors to provide additional capacity.

4. Maintain the present location and also build one or more new facilities.

5. Abandon the present location and build all new facilities elsewhere.

Analysis Methods

One way to make the location decision is to assign weights to the regional, community, and site factors considered important. Assigning individual weights for specific factors and totaling the weights for the various alternative sites may provide helpful insights for the location-selection decision.

Another approach is to make a *location break-even analysis*. First, the fixed and variable costs are identified for each alternative location (figure 3-1). Only relevant costs—those that differ from one location to the next and thus provide the basis for decision making—are included in the analysis. Next, the total-cost curves for each of the alternatives are plotted on a single graph (figure 3-2). Then, based on the forecasted level of activity, the alternative location with the lowest total cost is selected. For example, with expected volume VI in figure 3-2, alternative A is the most economical location.

When revenue also would be affected by the location site—for example, when a service operation has several possible location sites within a city—revenue curves would be added to the analysis. Then an evaluation would be conducted to determine the comparative profits based upon projected volumes at each potential site.

When a company with several plants and warehouses considers either adding capacity in one or more plants or relocating the territory served from each plant or warehouse, the transportation method of operations research may provide useful answers. This mathematical method shows the most economical pairing up of capacities of plants and warehouses with customer demand.

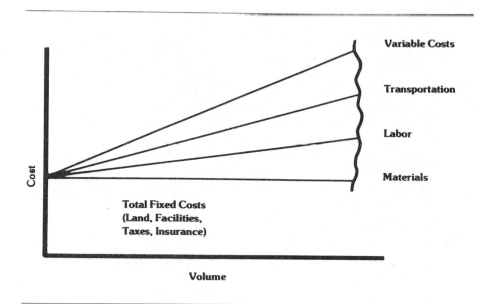

Figure 3-1.   Total Costs—Location A

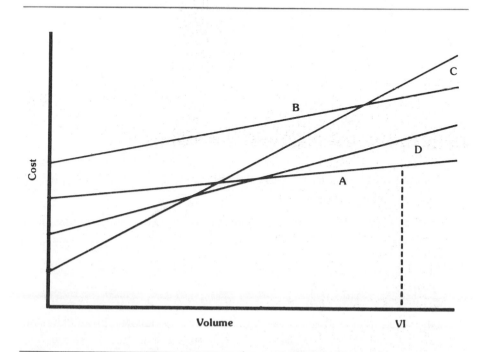

**Figure 3-2.   Total Costs for Alternative Locations
A, B, C, and D Compared to Volume**

Use of Consultants

A decision regarding location of facilities is made infrequently, and many managers never face this decision during their careers. Furthermore, the operations manager often will not have the final authority for making this decision; instead, it may be made by top management and usually involves the board of directors. The importance of the location decision, coupled with its infrequency, accounts for the use of specialized consultants when such decisions occur. Because these consultants normally are aware of the latest developments, better and faster location decisions are reached than if the firm relied solely on its own internal resources.

Facilities Layout

Facilities layout is the overall arrangement of machines, personnel, materials, handling, service facilities, and aisles required to facilitate efficient operation of the production system.

Several specific objectives of good facilities layout include:

1. Minimizing materials handling and plant transportation requirements. This reduces the costs and time to move materials through the production process and reduces work-in-process inventories.

2. Minimizing the amount of floor space required in order to maximize the return on the fixed investment in facilities. Floor congestion and production bottlenecks should be eliminated.

3. Utilizing labor efficiently and effectively by minimizing the distance and time to obtain materials, tools, and supplies; by facilitating maintenance and housecleaning; and by facilitating production supervision and use of support personnel.

4. Reducing the hazards affecting employees and products. Provision of adequate exhaust ducts, guard rails, and operating clearances makes the job safer.

5. Providing flexibility for expansion caused by growth, new products, and new processes.

The net effect should be to reduce work-in-process inventories, increase output, and reduce manufacturing unit costs.

Regardless of how effective the original layout is, changes are inevitable. Changes in demand, the introduction of new products, product-design changes, obsolescence of processes or equipment, changes in safety and personnel needs, and changes made to reduce costs all may prompt a re-layout.

Layout Patterns

Four basic layout patterns are used in manufacturing operations:

1.   Process layout

2.   Product or line layout

3.   Fixed-position layout

4.   Group or cellular layout

A *process layout,* which is used in the job-shop or intermittent-production system, groups all similar equipment together. For example, all drilling equipment would be in one area, all grinding equipment would be in another work center, and all milling equipment in still another. Figure 3-3 presents a graphic representation of a process layout. The variable-path nature of materials handling in process layouts eliminates much of the savings possible from the use of chutes, conveyors, or transfer machines.

The process layout is used where volume is low, several products are made, and processing flexibility is desired. General-purpose, low-cost machines generally are used. If one machine breaks down, the work usually can be shifted to other, similar machines. Because equipment in a process layout doesn't depend on a given sequence, machines that produce excessive noise,

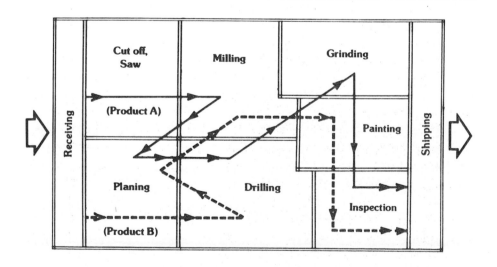

**Figure 3-3.   Process Layout Showing Movement
of Two Different Products**

vibration, fumes, or heat can be located in isolated areas. Since the work normally is paced by the employee rather than by the machines, individual incentive-pay systems can be used.

There are several disadvantages to the process layout: more complex planning and control because of routing, scheduling, and cost-accounting requirements; costlier materials handling; larger work-in-process inventories; increased storage and floor area requirements; increased costs for more skilled labor; more frequent inspection requirements; and more extensive supervision requirements.

A *product or line layout* arranges the equipment according to the progressive steps by which the product is made. Product layout is used in the continuous-production system where the number of end products is small, the parts are highly standardized and interchangeable, and the volume is large. Figure 3-4 presents a graphic representation of a product or line layout.

Product or line layout permits the use of costly, specialized, high-volume equipment; materials handling is simplified by means of transfer machines or conveyors; both production control and job training are easier; less inspection is required; there is less work-in-process; smaller aisles are required; and the floor area is more productive.

Disadvantages of the product or line layout include the higher initial equipment investment; greater vulnerability to work stoppage; the highly repetitive nature of the work; and the inflexibility that makes it more costly when changes are made due to product redesign.

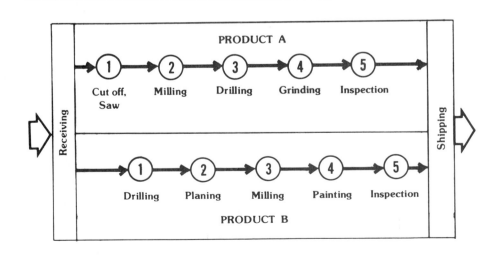

Figure 3-4. Product or Line Layout Showing
Movement of Two Different Products

With a *fixed-position layout,* the product remains in one position, due to its bulk or weight, and the workers, materials, and tools move to it. This layout normally is used in making items such as locomotives, ships, or large printing presses.

A *group or cellular layout* is indicated when a product is manufactured by means of group technology; that is, equipment and operations that have a common sequence for a family of parts or products are grouped together. This permits economic production of very small lots, thereby minimizing work-in-process inventories, space requirements, and production leadtimes. In layout by process, machines are grouped by type, and parts travel long distances between steps. By applying group technology with a cellular layout—that is, by combining several steps within an independent machining cell—production leadtime can be reduced, and less space is required. Figure 3-5 shows the differences between process layout and cellular layout.

Other types of layout include marketing, storage, yard, and office. A *marketing layout* is primarily arranged to facilitate the sale of products, such as in a supermarket. A *storage layout* is designed to fill an inventory and stock-keeping function, providing effective use of storage facilities and materials-handling equipment. A *yard layout* is used for outside storage, thereby reducing the need for inside facility requirements. An *office layout* facilitates the work of clerical and administrative employees.

Service organizations, such as banks, insurance companies, hospitals, restaurants, and offices, face many of the same layout problems as manufacturing organizations. The primary difference is that their facilities exist to bring the customers together with the organization's services. The layouts provide easy automobile entrance into parking areas from which sidewalks and well-marked entrances guide the customer into the service facility. Receiving or holding areas, cash registers, service counters, and employee work stations frequently are part of a service layout.

Service layouts receive and service the customer or process physical materials. A hospital, for example, may have a product or line layout for preparing serving trays; a process layout for various medical technologies, such as laboratory tests, radiology, and surgery; and a fixed-position layout within an operating room or intensive-care facility.

Restaurants also could have mixed layouts. For example, a buffet line would represent a product layout, and a seated dining area would represent a fixed-position layout. The kitchen itself, with its freezers, grills, ovens, dessert areas, and salad areas, represents a process layout.

In office automation and clerical applications, the primary considerations are the location and movement of people, paperwork, and equipment.

Before: Process Layout

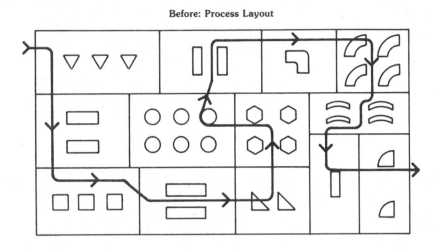

After: Cellular Layout

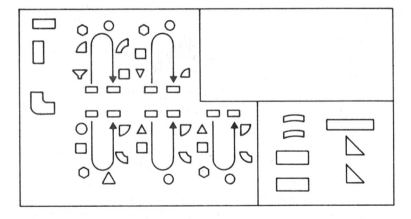

Figure 3-5. Layout by Process Versus Cellular Layout

Layout Cost Comparisons

As volume increases, the cost advantage moves successively from fixed-position layout, to process layout, to product layout. For this reason, many companies strive for high-volume operations to permit use of product layout in a continuous-production system.

In actual practice, most firms use a combination of layouts. For example, machining operations, even in large-volume operations such as those in the automobile industry, frequently are performed with a process layout. Automobile assembly operations, on the other hand, normally use a product or line layout pattern.

Layout Considerations

The layout analyst frequently starts the layout by locating the receiving and shipping departments, which are influenced by the location of rail lines, highways, and existing or potential dock facilities. Then the analyst must determine the size and shape of the other departments.

For process layouts, the primary consideration is minimizing materials-handling costs. A travel chart (figure 3-6) tabulates the frequency of loads between each of the departments. Multiplying the distance between each department by the number of loads moved provides a means of weighting the materials-handling cost. Loads below the diagonal line indicate undesirable backtracking. By rearranging the relative positions of the departments to obtain the greatest total weighting just above the diagonal line, the analyst develops various solutions before reaching the most satisfactory one.

For product layout, balance is the key criterion. Each step in the process should provide equal capacity so that material flow will be uninterrupted. With line-assembly operations, manpower should be assigned to each successive set of work stations so there will be a minimum of idle time in the assembly line. This process is called line balancing.

Within the actual production department, the analyst must provide adequate floor space for the man-machine interface, plus space for necessary

From					To			
	A	B	C	D	E	F	G	Total
A		40		15				55
B			50	10		22		82
C		5		55	15		5	80
D					55	15		70
E	15		10			25		50
F		5					30	35
G	10			15				25

Figure 3-6.   Travel Chart Used in Layout Planning

incoming and outgoing materials and access for maintenance service. Floor loads, ceiling heights, special plant utilities, dangerous operations, environmental problems (light, temperature, humidity, noise, vibration, and dirt), and safety (aisle widths and machine clearances) also must be considered.

Stockrooms, tool cribs, inspection stations, drinking fountains, and restrooms should be located to minimize the travel time for employees who will be using them. Locker rooms and washrooms should be located near where employees enter and leave the facility.

Flow-process charts and flow diagrams help determine the most effective patterns. The actual placement of machines, storage containers, and other equipment normally is decided after experimentally placing templates (two-dimensional cutouts) or three-dimensional scale models in position on a floor plan.

Materials Handling

Materials handling frequently is considered the twin of facilities layout because the type of materials-handling equipment utilized influences the plant layout and vice versa.

Materials-handling equipment is classified as either fixed-path or varied-path equipment. Fixed-path equipment (conveyors, chutes, cranes, and hoists) is relatively inflexible and handles material in large volume, normally in a continuous flow. Varied-path equipment (forklift trucks and four-wheel trucks) is flexible and normally handles materials in lots. Fixed-path equipment occupies space constantly, while varied-path equipment occupies space only intermittently.

Where variability is not required, there is a tendency to use fixed-path equipment for several reasons: (1) lower initial cost, (2) lower operating cost (no operator is required), (3) less supervision required, and (4) less space required.

A recent trend is to use automated materials-handling systems. Automatic storage and retrieval systems (AS/RS) place pallet loads within very large storage racks by means of automated stacking cranes. A computer locates an empty rack cell, directs the stacking crane to place the pallet within the rack, and then records the pallet's location for inventory purposes and automatic retrieval when desired. Robotic carriers automatically convey loads between the rack area and specified delivery areas by using wires installed in the floor to guide the carriers to their destination. These systems do not require operating personnel, and it is even possible to operate in total darkness.

Data Needed for Layout Planning

The layout analyst requires certain types of information. For example, the bill of materials (B/M) specifies the kinds of materials and parts required to make a unit of product (see chapter 2). This, coupled with the forecasted demand for end products and spare parts, helps determine the scale of operations. In addition, the analyst must know the sequence of operations for processing and assembling parts into the end product. A master route sheet helps in making these determinations. With information concerning the products, product mix, market demand, and work standards, the analyst can determine the number and kinds of machines and tooling systems required and proceed to make an effective layout.

Computerized Methods

Use of the travel chart is not feasible when many departments are involved, so computers may be used to help make layout decisions. The computer utilizes heuristic or algorithmic techniques for line balancing in product and process layout. Operations research techniques used for layout purposes are simulation and queuing theory. For example, queuing theory could help determine how many shipping or receiving docks should be built, how many fork trucks are required, and how many tool-crib attendants are needed to provide service to the workers.

Equipment Types and Their Selection

Equipment affects labor requirements, quality control, production capacity, and job design. Selection of equipment is based primarily on the product/ services design, product/services volume, quality requirements, and cost considerations.

Firms must determine whether a specific type of work requires general-purpose machines or special-purpose machines. General-purpose machines— lathes or drill presses, for example—are capable of handling a variety of jobs. On the other hand, special-purpose machines, such as an automated transfer line, usually are faster and more efficient, but changing these complex systems to handle different product designs is difficult and costly.

General-purpose machines, compared to special-purpose machines, are less costly, have a broad range of job applications, are relatively simple to maintain, and have less obsolescence. On the other hand, they usually have slower operating rates, are less productive, have less consistent quality, and involve large work-in-process inventories. Special-purpose machines are extremely costly and normally are used only for high-volume production.

Numerical-control (N/C) machines are general-purpose machines that are most costly but faster and more efficient. Such machines are preprogrammed, by means of alphanumeric instructions on punched paper tape or magnetic tape, to perform a cycle of operations repetitively. Since production is almost automatic, labor costs are reduced because a single operator often can operate several machines at the same time. Quality is improved and is more consistent.

Tooling costs and lead time requirements also are reduced considerably. The primary disadvantages of N/C machines are their higher initial cost, the need for specially trained programmers, and higher maintenance costs.

Automated batch manufacturing systems (ABMS) or transfer machines are superior to N/C machines where large volumes are involved. Parts are attached to a conveying system and carried through a system of individual machines that transforms the parts into finished units. All product handling is eliminated, except at the first and last operations. In one early installation, 42 machines were connected to perform 530 operations required to machine engine blocks. The ABMS reduced time from nine hours per block to less than 15 minutes.

Computer-aided manufacturing (CAM) is a sophisticated extension of direct numerical control of machine tools, robots, and inspection machines. Ideally, CAM interfaces with computer-aided design (see chapter 2). Data bases developed by CAD are used to manufacture tooling, program tooling for N/C machines, and program inspection machines in the development of CAM applications. In the future, information may pass directly from CAD to CAM via the data base with minimal use of engineering drawings. The CAD/CAM linkage greatly shortens the time between design and production. For example, in designing and making hydraulic tubing for aircraft, one manufacturer reduced manpower from 12 to 3 persons; time from release of the drawing to finished product was reduced from six weeks to 18 minutes.

Industrial robots are increasingly used for highly repetitive manual jobs. The robots are computer controlled and usually are programmed initially by being hand guided through the required operation. Their greatest disadvantage is the initial cost; however, their operating costs usually are low, and they are easy to reprogram for other jobs. Robots are reliable in operation and eliminate problems of employee absenteeism and tardiness. Because of its labor shortages, Japan uses considerably more robots than any other country.

Capital Investments

Capital investments in machinery, equipment, and research and development are important because they are long-term commitments to expense reduction and revenue generation. Thus, they affect the firm's solvency, fundraising requirements, competitive capability, and overall performance. Capital expenditures are required not only to outfit the facility initially but also to expand capacity and replace worn-out or obsolete equipment.

The most common methods of ranking equipment alternatives are payback, net present value, and return on investment (ROI).

Payback ranks investments according to the time required for each investment to return earnings equal to the cost of the investment. The rationale is that the faster an investment can recover its cost, the greater the capital turnover rate, meaning that the firm will gain the most benefit from its available investment funds. The interest in the payback method comes from the desire for liquidity of funds.

Net present value determines the amount by which the present value of a projected income stream exceeds the cost of the investment. Decisions are made by comparing the net value of future earnings from each machine being evaluated.

Return on investment (ROI) focuses on the percentage rate of return on the investment. Obviously, the rate of return should exceed the cost of borrowing money.

Most concerns make their equipment-investment decisions using the payback method combined with one of the other methods. When choosing among investment proposals, firms often regard tax considerations (and investment tax credits) as the deciding factor because depreciation expenses directly affect taxable income and profits.

Maintenance

Maintenance operations include all efforts to keep production facilities and equipment in proper operating condition. The four types of maintenance operations are: (1) breakdown repair, (2) millwright (men who move and install equipment) activities and minor construction, (3) preventive maintenance, and (4) custodial services. Breakdown and millwright are called irregular maintenance because the demands for such services occur at irregular intervals and impose variable loads on the maintenance department. Preventive and custodial may be called regular or periodic maintenance for they may be performed on a set schedule.

Much attention has been given to the proper relationship of breakdown repair versus preventive maintenance. Breakdown repair is a special problem because breakdowns are random, creating peaks and valleys in the work load. Queuing theory and Monte Carlo simulation (two specialized operation research techniques) are methods of analyzing breakdown waiting lines and distributions to determine personnel and scheduling requirements. In any case, the uneven maintenance work load may cause the maintenance department to operate inefficiently. However, in the interest of maximizing performance of the manufacturing departments, the firm may decide to accept some inefficiencies in the operation of the maintenance department.

Preventive maintenance (PM) is performed before the equipment breaks down so that it continues to operate satisfactorily and reduces the likelihood of breakdown. Its primary advantages are that it enables maintenance crews to schedule their time evenly, tends to minimize equipment breakdowns, and may be scheduled to avoid work stoppages. PM schedules may be based on calendar time or equipment usage time. To function successfully, a good PM program depends upon records, which include a maintenance history for each piece of equipment. These permit analysis of breakdown frequency and causes, thereby providing a basis for improving the PM procedure.

Two modifications of a PM program designed to reduce costs are group replacement and standby equipment. Group replacement applies to a large group of identical components, such as light bulbs. Analysis based on failure-probability distribution may justify replacing components after a certain time, along with units that already have failed, rather than replacing the units individually as they fail. In standby equipment analysis, the minimum total cost between the costs of lost service due to out-of-service machines versus the costs of keeping extra machines on hand to avoid a shutdown is sought.

Centralized maintenance departments are appropriate for small plants, but in large plants much time would be wasted by maintenance personnel traveling to the job site. An alternative is to have maintenance personnel assigned to specific areas. Area maintenance also permits better knowledge of the equipment, develops a greater sense of responsibility, and permits faster response time to problems.

Energy Management

Energy is one of the major purchased resources most firms use. Since the oil crunch of the early 1970s, the high costs of oil and petroleum derivatives have focused much more attention on energy management. Energy sources such as coal, nuclear power, hydrogenerated electricity, wood, the sun, geo-thermal heat, shale oil, and wind are possible energy alternatives. Government programs and tax incentives now encourage investments in energy-conserving devices and materials, such as more efficient motors or insulating materials.

Many firms now have formal energy-management programs (EMP). Such programs start with an audit to determine an organization's current energy utilization. The gross energy audit measures total energy consumption and identifies the types of energy used. A detailed energy audit determines how much of each type of energy is being used and where (i.e., which process, operations, or machines).

Energy-management programs seek improvements through several types of conservation methods: (1) process changes, (2) product changes, (3) materials conservation, (4) heat-recovery applications, (5) improved equipment controls, (6) housekeeping practices, and (7) facilities design and insulation. Through these programs, many firms actually have reduced their energy requirements even in the face of organization growth.

Safety and OSHA

Worker safety is an important factor in job design. Accidents are expensive and include such direct costs as worker's compensation and medical and legal costs, plus such indirect costs as machine downtime, material waste, lost production, equipment damage, and worker training and replacement costs.

Safe and healthful working conditions are important, and managers should respond to this problem with planned safety programs. The responsibility for carrying out a safety program should be spelled out for both supervisory and higher management levels. The success of any safety program depends primarily upon the first-line supervisor; however, the supervisor's role is easier if the program is backed by top management. Management can demonstrate support of safety programs by attending safety meetings, delegating authority to make on-the-spot corrections of unsafe acts and conditions, taking quick action when safety hazards or violations become evident, and making funds available to provide a safe working environment. Workers, too, must become involved and impressed with their responsibility for their own safety and the safety of their coworkers. Worker involvement can be achieved through safety training and education—for example, teaching workers the proper way to lift objects and the benefits of wearing protective clothing. Under the Occupational Safety and Health Act (OSHA), management is responsible for workers injured while not wearing management provided equipment unless management can clearly document attempts to enforce such use by disciplinary methods, including discharge.

Most accidents involve unsafe conditions, unsafe acts, or both. Unsafe conditions pertain to machines, materials-handling equipment, maintenance, layout, and housekeeping. Machine hazards exist when moving parts are not enclosed or equipped with guards. Forklift trucks may injure the operator or hit someone else. Lack of maintenance can cause failures of brakes, steering, tires, cables, or steam valves. Improper layout may cause accidents because of narrow aisles, overhanging obstacles, or blind corners. Poor housekeeping can cause fires or falls.

Unsafe acts account for as much as 90 percent of all accidents. Workers often feel that accidents only happen to someone else. They must be trained to be alert to hazards and ways to avoid injury. For example, the large number of painful and costly back injuries could be minimized if workers learned to lift with their leg muscles rather than their back muscles.

OSHA was passed by Congress at the urging of labor groups and took effect in 1971. Under the act, OSHA inspectors may visit a firm on their own initiative, or they may be requested by a union or an employee to investigate a problem. The company cannot take disciplinary measures against a complainant. Violation of OSHA standards may involve fines up to $10,000 or up to six months in jail (for willful violations causing death) or fines of

$1,000 per day (for failure to correct cited violations). Recent legal actions suggest that a manager who knowingly tolerates unsafe working conditions that result in the death of a worker may be charged with murder.

Prior to OSHA, safety efforts were directed almost completely at reducing accidents. Little attention was directed at job-induced health impairment. Currently, OSHA is placing increased emphasis upon work environments that involve coke making, chemicals like polyvinyl chloride, certain insecticides, asbestos, beryllium, and other dangerous materials.

Noise reduction also has received considerable emphasis under OSHA. Prolonged exposure to excessive noise not only ultimately will impair a person's hearing but also may induce high blood pressure, stress, and headaches. OSHA regulations say exposure to average noise levels of 90 decibels or over for eight hours or longer probably is injurious to most people. Unless noise is reduced to the prescribed levels, companies must supply workers with ear plugs or earmuffs or reduce the exposure time. Annual hearing tests are mandatory if workers are continually exposed to an average of 85 decibels or more.

Work Study

In the broadest sense, every organization is concerned with providing goods or offering services while utilizing men and women, machines, materials, and facilities as resources. All operating units should be concerned with performing their work more effectively, efficiently, and economically. Work study is a useful way to coordinate and utilize available resources effectively.

Work study usually is divided into two parts: work design and work measurement. Work design means finding the most effective method of doing a job. It involves analyzing present and preferred work systems to develop an optimal transformation of resource inputs into the desired product or service outputs. Work measurement determines how long it should take a qualified and trained employee working at a normal pace to do a specific task or operation, with due allowances for fatigue and personal and unavoidable delays. Work study also is known as motion and time study.

Although work design and work measurement can be used independently, it is not desirable to establish measured time standards of operations if the operations are not being performed efficiently. In short, work design is a prerequisite to effective work measurement. Otherwise, the measurement only portrays "what is" rather than "what should be."

Wage incentives are a further extension of a work-study program. Incentive programs may involve any one of many plans where an individual or group receives additional direct pay, a bonus, or profit sharing based on performance in relation to work standards established through work measurement.

Under an incentive program, workers should minimize delays within their control, supervisors should improve the planning and coordination of re-sources, and workers should put forth additional effort to obtain the incentive offered.

Benefits

The financial and competitive pressures on today's manager greatly increase the need for work study. Specifically, work design analysis should result in greater productivity through improved methods that normally permit an in-creased output with the same or less effort. Additional benefits often include reduction in worker fatigue; improved work-place layout, product design, materials handling, and tooling; and increased safety. Work-measurement standards may be used for planning work and determining schedules; deter-mining standard costs; line balancing and machine effectiveness rating; de-termining time standards as a basis for incentive wages; and establishing a formal performance-reporting system.

In the long run, the most secure manager or employee is the one who works for the most progressive and cost-effective procedure. Work study is an effective management tool for obtaining this goal.

Work Design

There are several prerequisites for work improvement:

1. Large-scale, repetitive production
2. Standardization of all factors materially affecting job performance, such as the product, materials, process, layout, materials handling, working environment, and methods and motion
3. Possession of know-how, creativity, and a questioning attitude
4. Support of top management and supervisors

   Work-design analysis is applied in three separate phases:

1. Analysis of the initial design of the product and its processing
2. Periodic reviews of an apparently satisfactory existing method to see if further improvement might be made
3. Special studies made when problems arise due to changed or special circumstances

Process Charts—Interstation Analysis

An organization's work is based on a flow that connects a series of chro-nological steps performed by individuals at various work stations. Such work may be analyzed by several types of charts. These charts utilize special symbols to designate specific functions so the analyst can show consistently what is happening with the present method before preparing a chart of the proposed improved method. Besides being useful analysis tools, charts also aid in explaining and selling proposed changes to management and the employees concerned.

The five commonly used charts are: (1) flow-process chart, (2) flow diagram, (3) assembly-flow process, or gozinto, chart, (4) operation-process chart, and (5) office-procedure flow chart.

The American Society of Mechanical Engineers' (ASME) standardized set of five symbols are most commonly used in constructing process charts:

1. A large circle ◯ denotes an *operation*.
2. An arrow ▷ denotes a *transportation* or movement of worker or material over three feet.
3. A square ☐ denotes an *inspection* for quality or quantity.
4. A large letter D denotes a *delay*.
5. An inverted triangle ▽ indicates a *storage*.

In a flow-process chart (figure 3-7), the chronological steps in the process are listed along with the approximate times and distances and remarks pertinent to each item listed. The chart must follow *either* the worker *or* the material.

After charting the proposed method, the analyst uses the following approaches to develop a better method:

1. Eliminates all unnecessary work
2. Combines operations or elements
3. Changes the sequence of operations, the place, or the person
4. Simplifies the remaining necessary operations

Since a questioning attitude is essential in methods improvement, a good start may be made by asking: What? Who? When? Where? How? And each question should be coupled with the question Why? Experience and check lists then will provide further, specific questions—for example, are specified tolerances too close? Could molded, cast, or forged parts be substituted to eliminate machining or other operations?

A flow diagram uses the symbols connected by arrows on a floor plan to depict the flow of the process (figure 3-8). The process chart symbols may be used to prepare an assembly-flow process, or gozinto, chart, which shows the work flow for the different purchased and manufactured parts through assembly and into the finished product (figure 3-9). An operation-process

Present Method ⊠ ;   Proposed Method ☐

Subject charted: *Manufacture mounting bracket*   Date *Dec. 3, 1985*

Begins: *Receiving Department*   Charted by   *J. Jones*

Ends: *Finished Stores Department*   Page *1* of *1*

Step	Symbol	Distance	Time	Description
1	⇨	40'	15 min	Received from delivery truck
2	☐	–	5 min	Inspected
3	⇨	40'	5 min	To raw material stores
4	▽	–		In raw material stores
5	⇨	60'	10 min	Truck to cut-off saws
6	D			Wait at saws
7	◯		30 min	Cut to size
8	D			Wait for truck
9	⇨	60'	5 min	Truck to drills
10	◯		5 min	Drill 2 holes
11	⇨	120'	10 min	Truck to assembly
12	D			Wait for assembly
13	◯		10 min	Assembly
14	☐		2 min	Inspect assembly
15	⇨	60'	5 min	Truck to finished stores
16	▽			In finished stores inventory

Figure 3-7.   Flow-Process Chart

chart resembles the assembly-process chart except that it is simplified and uses only two symbols—operation and inspection. Although the flow-process chart can be used successfully to analyze certain office operations, an office-process flow chart is used to follow the flow of the multiple copies involved in many types of paperwork systems.

Intrastation Analysis

Methods analysis first should be made of the overall operations—that is, interstation—with a process chart. Then the remaining operations are subjected to an intrastation analysis to further simplify and improve the work.

Intrastation techniques basically involve two main categories: (1) a worker-and-machine chart or multiple-activity chart and (2) an operation analysis.

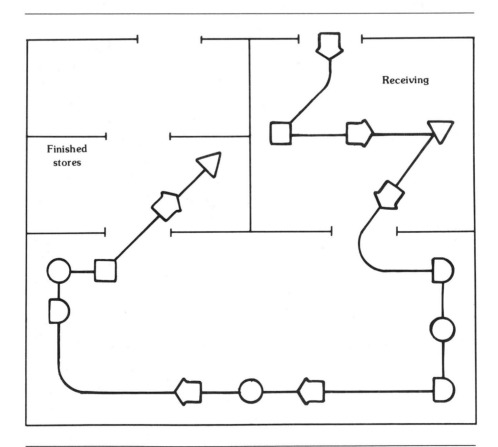

Figure 3-8.   Flow Diagram

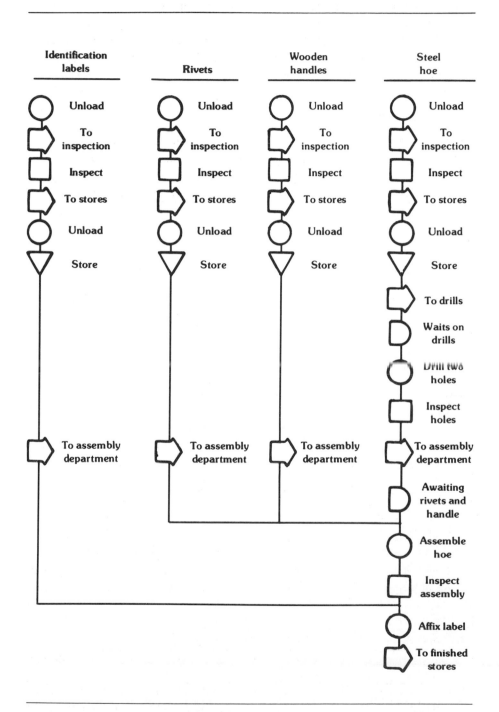

Figure 3-9.   Assembly Process Chart (Garden Hoe)

When one worker is utilizing one machine, the worker-and-machine chart is used against a time scale to portray graphically the breakdown of the movements involved. When one or more workers are operating one or more machines, the activity of each worker or machine is depicted on a separate column against the time scale needed to complete the work cycle. This is called a multiple-activity chart (figure 3-10).

Each step in the chart is then subjected to the questions previously described. The objective is to minimize the idle time for the worker and/or the machine. For example, idle worker time can be reduced by rearranging certain operations, including additional work, or giving the worker additional equipment to handle. When the operations of a group of workers must be coordinated, the multiple-activity chart is an effective analysis technique.

The operation, or right-hand/left-hand, chart (figure 3-11) analyzes how the worker utilizes both hands during the work cycle. Again, it is necessary first to portray the present method and analyze the steps within the function to develop an improved method. The same or similar symbols may be used as in the flow-process chart.

When Frank and Lillian Gilbreth devised the operation chart, they also devised certain principles of motion economy. These principles or guides refer not only to the movement of the worker but also to the arrangement of the work place and to the design of the tools and equipment.

To provide an even more detailed analysis of the hand movement, the Gilbreths developed therblig analysis and micromotion study. Therbligs are 17 fundamental movements or actions, such as transport empty, grasp, transport loaded, release load, and hold. Therblig symbols are used in constructing the detailed motion charts for analysis.

The Gilbreths also were pioneers in the use of the motion picture camera for making therblig analyses to describe basic elements of work. By either counting the frames on a constant-speed camera or by using a special clock called a microchronometer, an analyst can make an accurate and detailed study of right- and left-hand motions of the worker. This information then is plotted against a time scale on a simultaneous motion-cycle chart (simo chart) to provide a readily visible time relationship of the therbligs to each other. Memo-motion (50-100 frames per minute, versus 960-1,000 frames per minute with a conventional movie camera) or time-lapse photography (frames at specified time intervals) permits analysis of operations at greatly reduced cost for film and the analyst's time.

Work-Distribution Chart

The work-distribution charting technique is an excellent way to determine the work tasks performed and the respective time taken by each individual worker. First, each worker prepares a task list or time ladder, recording both

Subject: *Operating Two Broaching Machines*   Date *Dec. 3, 1985*

Present ☒ ; Proposed ☐   Department: *Broaching*   Charted by *V.M.R.*

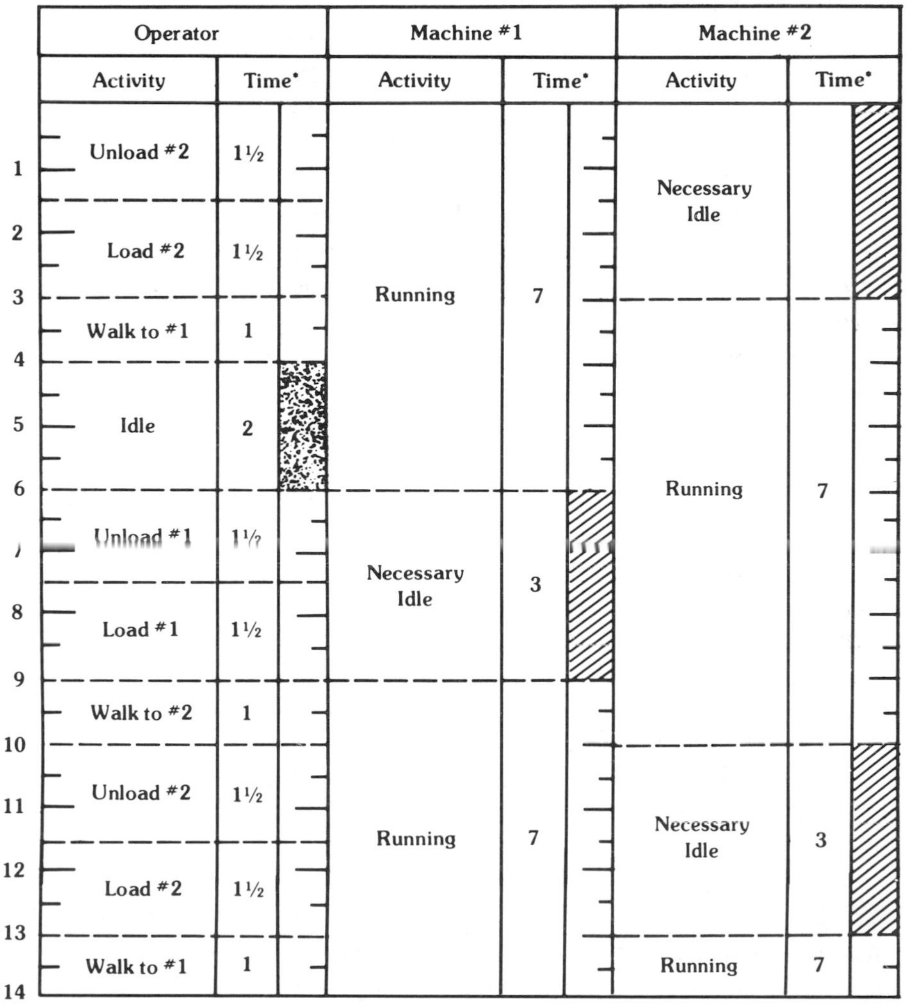

	Operator			Machine #1			Machine #2	
	Activity	Time*		Activity	Time*		Activity	Time*
1	Unload #2	1½		Running	7		Necessary Idle	
2	Load #2	1½						
3	Walk to #1	1					Running	7
4								
5	Idle	2						
6				Necessary Idle	3			
⁊	Unload #1	1½						
8	Load #1	1½						
9	Walk to #2	1		Running	7			
10	Unload #2	1½					Necessary Idle	3
11								
12	Load #2	1½						
13	Walk to #1	1					Running	7
14								

Figure 3-10.   Multiple-Activity Chart

the time taken for performing each separate type of task throughout the day and the number of units processed. Periodically (normally, weekly), this information is summarized. After sample data are collected for a typical work cycle (week, month, or quarter), an activities chart is constructed showing

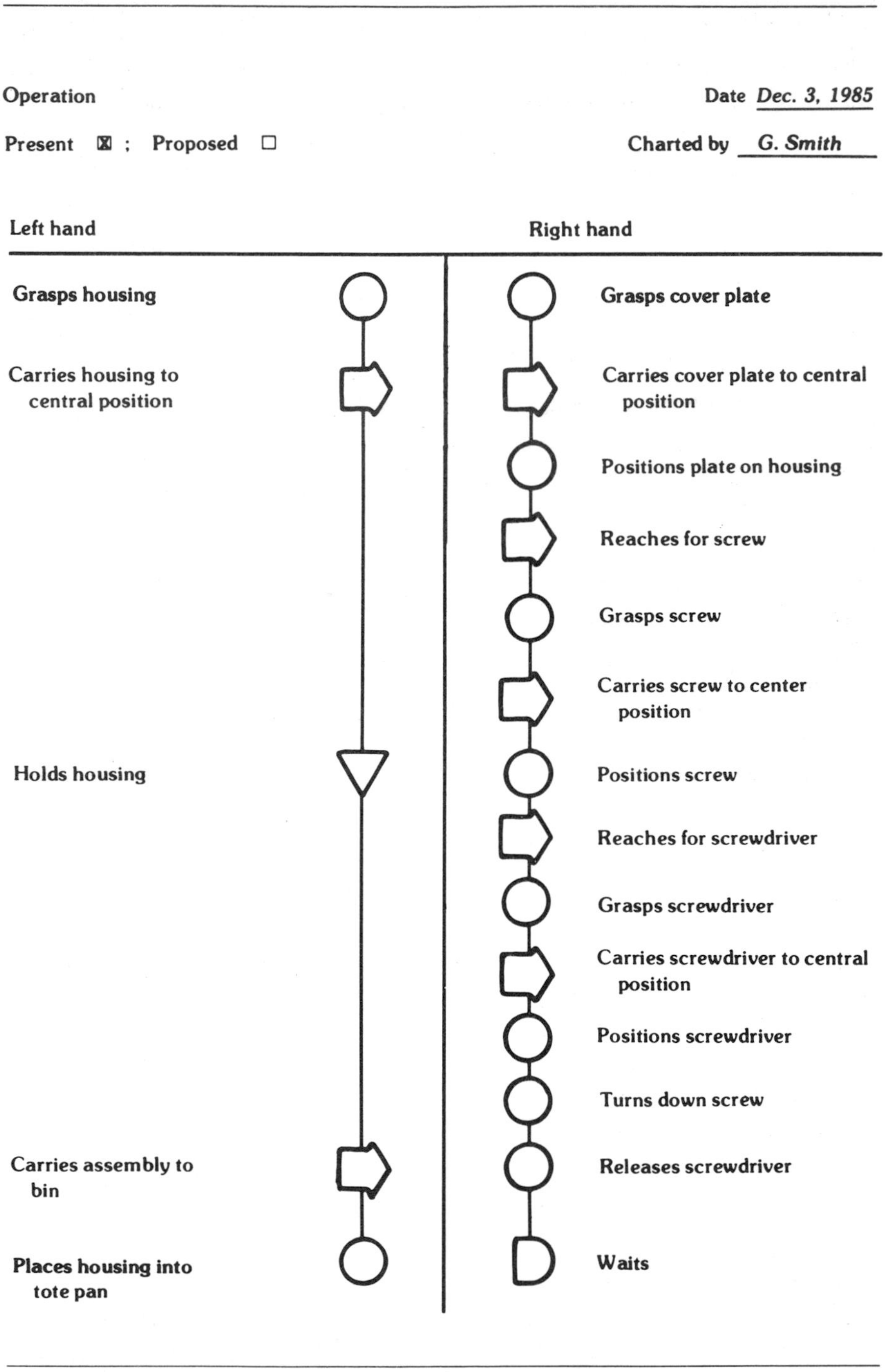

Operation   Date *Dec. 3, 1985*

Present ☒ ;   Proposed ☐   Charted by   *G. Smith*

Left hand		Right hand
Grasps housing	◯ ⎮ ◯	**Grasps cover plate**
Carries housing to central position	⬠ ⎮ ⬠	Carries cover plate to central position
	◯	Positions plate on housing
	⬠	Reaches for screw
	◯	Grasps screw
	⬠	Carries screw to center position
Holds housing	▽ ◯	Positions screw
	⬠	Reaches for screwdriver
	◯	Grasps screwdriver
	⬠	Carries screwdriver to central position
	◯	Positions screwdriver
	◯	Turns down screw
Carries assembly to bin	⬠ ◯	Releases screwdriver
Places housing into tote pan	◯ ⎮ D	Waits

Figure 3-11.   Operation Chart

each task related to a major activity, and the activities are ranked based on hours utilized. A work-distribution chart is constructed on the basis of the summarized task list and the activity list. The various activities with their associated tasks are listed against the respective time requirements for each member of the group. Careful vertical, horizontal, and overall analysis of the work-distribution chart should suggest areas for improvement.

Work Measurement

Several methods are used to establish work-output standards:

1.   Estimates based on historical data

2.   Stopwatch time studies

3.   Predetermined motion-time standards

4.   Elemental data

5.   Work sampling

Estimates Based on Historical Data

Work standards in some organizations are based solely upon experience estimates or past recorded performance. Such standards suffer, however, for several reasons:

1.   They do not reflect methods arrived at through work-design efforts.

2.   The jobs are not standardized and may reflect a variety of methods.

3.   There is no suitable measure of the performance levels.

4.   They do not reflect accurate methods of timing and recording the data.

The other techniques are more accurate. If applied by qualified personnel, they offer improved results that increase production and lower costs. Also, they are more satisfactory to both the employee and the employer.

Work design of the methods, to include standardized work conditions, should precede work-measurement studies; otherwise, the work standards are meaningless. In any case, the work measurements should be revised as work methods improve.

Stopwatch Time Study

The most common approach to work measurement involves a stopwatch time study, which incorporates a performance rating of the operation to determine its normal time requirements. The equipment for making time studies consists of a decimal minute stopwatch, an observation sheet, and a special clipboard.

To insure use of improved and standardized working conditions, qualified operators must be trained in these standardized methods. The time-study person operates in a staff capacity and works closely with supervisors and employees to insure that job conditions are proper and as specified in the pertinent job documentation. The operation then is broken down into smaller units called elements, which provide the basis for obtaining time data. The analyst observes and records the actual time required for the elements, while also making a performance rating. Statistical formulae, alignment charts, and the analyst's judgment may be used to determine the number of observations required to yield the desired precision. Upon completing the observations, the analyst multiplies the average observed time by the performance rating to obtain the normal time. Allowances for personal time, unavoidable delays, and fatigue are factored into the normal time to obtain the standard time required to complete each element. By adding the standard times for each element, the analyst then obtains the standard time for the work cycle or piece (assuming one piece produced per cycle). By dividing the standard time into the minutes for the period (hour or day), the analyst then obtains a production standard for that time period.

Predetermined Motion-Time Study

Predetermined Motion-Time Study (PMTS) is a synthetic time study that permits the development of time standards without anyone actually observing the worker doing a particular task, providing the motion pattern is known. It also enables the audit of establised time standards.

PMTS systems are developed by means of data gathered primarily through motion picture cameras or special electronic timing equipment. Tables of basic data are compiled that represent normal time for selected motions, and it is not necessary to utilize performance ratings. The two most widely used PMTS systems are methods-time-measurement (MTM) and work-factor. It is important that PMTS data be applied only by well-trained people.

Elemental Data

Frederick Taylor established the use of elemental data to reduce the cost and time of establishing work standards. Certain kinds of work have several common work elements; for example, some kinds of machine-tool work may be virtually alike except for the machining or cutting time. Consequently, by conducting work-design studies for the entire class of similar work and then developing tables of standard data for the common elements, it is possible to establish a time standard faster and more economically than if each such job were studied individually.

The tables of elemental data may be constructed from data developed by means of either time study or PMTS.

Work Sampling

Work sampling is based on probability theory and involves observing a sample of the work activity. The number of observations required will vary, depending on the activity and the desired degree of accuracy. Work sampling may be used to determine allowances, develop performance ratings, or obtain time standards without use of a stopwatch. Work sampling is particularly useful in analyzing long and irregular work cycles, such as those in a shipping department or office.

Limitations of Work Study and Work Measurement

Work study and work measurement are subject to certain limitations, including the following:

1. They must involve physical work that can be seen.

2. They are more suitable for manual work than machine-paced operations.

3. They will require stricter enforcement of quality standards, especially if wage incentives are in effect.

4. Unions may oppose work measurement, especially stopwatch time study. Consequently, the time-study person must be not only a skilled technical researcher but also a diplomat.

The success of any manufacturing firm is based only in part on the design and development of new products. Of equal importance is the efficiency of the organization in producing the product within quality, value, and cost standards that enhance the profitability of that product. Although work study historically has been associated primarily with production work, the principles are universal. Consequently, work design and work measurement are being applied increasingly to nonproduction and clerical activities.

Job Design

Job design specifies the work activities of an individual or group in an organization. The objective is to meet the requirements of the organization, the technology, and the worker. Job specialization, job enlargement, and job enrichment are the three primary approaches to job design.

Job specialization (division of labor) has made possible high-speed, low-cost production and has greatly enhanced our standard of living. It is generally conceded that the short work cycles required with specialization are very productive and require less skilled labor, less training, less supervision, and less tooling. Many people actually prefer a repetitive type of work. But the behaviorists have contended that job enlargement and job enrichment lead to a less monotonous, more productive, and more satisfying job for the worker.

The introduction of more variety in work—that is, a wider range of assembly operations—creates horizontal loading or *job enlargement*. The addition of one or more responsibilities—that is, work design (develop methods and workplace layout), identity (complete work on an entire item), autonomy (control of scheduling), or inspection and testing (control of quality)—results in vertical job loading or *job enrichment*.

Since its inception with IBM in 1950, job enrichment has been credited with many instances of reduced absenteeism, less turnover, improved quality, greater work satisfaction, and, in some cases, improved productivity. In other instances, productivity is less than with specialization, and the question is whether the tradeoffs are desirable. Many workers prefer specialization. As an example, the seniority distribution of an assembly-line work force frequently is grouped at either end of the spectrum: some of these workers prefer specialization and have been on the line many years, while others dislike specialization and soon either will terminate or transfer to other jobs.

Variable work schedules such as flextime, four-workday weeks, permanent part-time jobs, and job sharing are also means of making the job more attractive.

Wage-Payment Plans

Pay systems usually are based on payment for time *or* for output. Payment by time, called day work, normally is by the hour. This is easy to understand and calculate. All workers in a given job will be paid the same amount per hour—regardless of output levels. There is little incentive to work hard in such a situation. In fact, a person who works too fast often is subjected to social pressure to conform to the group norm.

Payment by output is a form of incentive pay. Most workers who are given a chance to earn more by producing more do so. The most common wage-incentive plans for direct labor usually are based on output compared to work standards set through work measurement. The starting points for incentive-pay systems are job base rates and production standards. The base rate is established by some form of job-evaluation plan. The production standards are set by work measurement, such as stopwatch time study or a predetermined time system.

The simplest type of wage incentive plan is piece work, which pays the worker a stated amount per unit produced. Since there is no guaranteed base rate, the plan is not common today because of federal minimum wage requirements.

The standard hour plan is the most common wage-incentive plan used today. Pay for the period is calculated by multiplying the base rate times the number of standard hours of output produced during the period. The employee is guaranteed the daily base wage. This plan also is called the one-for-one or 100 percent premium plan because the employee is paid 100 percent of all the good units produced above standard.

Incentive-pay plans also may be applied to groups of employees. The Lincoln Electric and Scanlon plans, which share productivity gains with employees, are two of the better known versions.

Accurate work standards are necessary for the operation of successful wage and incentive plans. If standards are too loose, workers will be achieving their incentives bonuses too easily, and they may restrict output to avoid attracting the attention of management to the incorrect rate. Also, a standard that is too tight will cause employee complaints and will not motivate effectively.

When operations, materials, and products change, the standard should be modified to reflect these changes. In addition, audits should be conducted to verify that the standards in current use still are accurate. The failure to audit and correct standards when changes occur is the major reason wage-incentive programs deteriorate.

One problem with wage-incentive systems is that quantity may be stressed at the expense of quality. This may be overcome by paying the worker at the incentive rate only for those items of acceptable quality. When properly designed, installed, and maintained, incentive plans normally will increase productivity; increase employees' earnings; reduce costs for equipment, facilities, and fringe benefits; and make the organization more competitive.

Cost Reduction

In recent years, a company's financial report of increased revenue often has been tempered by a statement that either net earnings are down or they have not kept pace with the rate of revenue increase. Several forces have been primarily responsible: (1) the increase in the costs of labor, materials, and services; (2) intensified domestic and foreign competition; and (3) government regulation.

Today, serious and continuing attention to costs is vital. For the modern manager, the methods and techniques of cost control and cost reduction are not supplementary skills; cost control and cost cutting should be a way of life rather than a panic reaction to an economic slump.

Several factors are needed to provide a successful cost-control and cost-reduction program: (1) the active support of top management, (2) assurance that jobs will not be lost because of improvements, (3) cost-reduction goals, (4) current status reports of progress, (5) announcements of savings, (6) frequent review of the program by management, (7) continuation of cost-reduction programs when business is good, and (8) follow-up to ensure successful implementation of plans.

Participation is a useful technique in cost-reduction programs, and *all* employees can contribute ideas. Cost-reduction committees are helpful if organized with top-management support. The committee sets a positive climate, exerts social pressure for constructive action, gathers information for status and progress reports, and coordinates plans for cost-reduction programs.

Of the many cost-reduction techniques, a few representative types are: (1) work simplification, (2) performance improvement, (3) value engineering/value analysis, (4) profit improvement, and (5) suggestion systems. The key to cost-reduction programs is mental attitude. Creative thinking continually seeks easier and more effective, efficient, and economical ways to do the job.

References

Barnes, Ralph M. *Motion and Time Study: Design and Measurement of Work.* 7th ed. New York: John Wiley & Sons, 1980.

Chase, Richard B., and Aquilano, Nicholas J. *Production and Operations Management.* 4th ed. Homewood, IL: Richard D. Irwin, 1985.

Hendrick, Thomas E., and Moore, Franklin G. *Production/Operations Management.* 9th ed. Homewood, IL: Richard D. Irwin, 1985.

Hopeman, Richard J. *Production: Concepts, Analysis and Control.* 4th ed. Columbus, OH: Charles E. Merrill, 1980.

Riggs, James L. *Production Systems: Planning, Analysis and Control,* 3rd ed. New York: John Wiley & Sons, 1981.

Schonberger, Richard J. *Operations Management.* 2nd ed. Plano, TX: Business Publications, Inc., 1985.

Discussion Questions

1. a. Discuss the three phases involved in the facilities-location decision.
    b. Name the regional factors involved.

2. What are the advantages and disadvantages of city versus rural location?

3. a. Name the four primary layout patterns used in manufacturing operations.
    b. What are the advantages and disadvantages of process layout versus product or line layout?

4. Name and briefly describe several types of manufacturing equipment

5. Discuss the need for and approaches to equipment maintenance.

6. How does OSHA contribute to worker safety?

7. Name and briefly discuss several types of analysis charts used in work study.

8. Explain why the term *work measurement* is more comprehensive and realistic than the term *time study*.

9. Name and compare several types of wage-payment plans.

Chapter 4

Forecasting, Planning, and Scheduling Production

So far, we have explored how a product is designed and the steps necessary to get both the product and physical facility ready for actual production. This chapter discusses how the demand for a product is determined and then, based upon this demand, how the actual production is planned and the required resources are scheduled.

These three activities are closely tied together in a hierarchical arrangement, with forecasting at the top, followed by planning, and then scheduling. This means that if the demand forecast changes, the production plan probably will have to be adjusted, and the scheduling of resources also must be altered to reflect the new plan.

Forecasting Demand

The basis for all business activity is a forecast of demand, which indicates the venture will be profitable. Perfect forecasts, however, are rare. Realizing this, the forecaster must make an effort to develop forecasts that represent the best estimates of future demand. The five basic steps to be reviewed are: (1) determining the forecasting objective, (2) selecting a model, (3) assessing the proposed model, (4) applying the model that passes initial assessment, and (5) monitoring the performance of the model to determine the justification of continued use of the selected model.

Determining the Objective

The forecaster actually must forecast *two* types of demand—internal and external.

Internal, or dependent, demand is derived from or contingent on the demand for some other product or item. Raw materials, components, and subassemblies are examples of items subject to internal demand; that is, they are dependent upon the demand for the final product. The paper used in printing this text is dependent upon the demand for this and other texts to be printed. This paper raw material faces only an internal demand as specified by a detailed component list of materials required to manufacture various books (the bill of materials, see chapter 2).

Since the bill of materials for a product indicates, in detail, the requirements for items facing internal demands, the forecaster also must be concerned with external demands. External demands, which are unrelated to the demands for other items produced by the firm, also are known as independent demands. Items that have independent or external demands usually are end products or items used for maintenance and repair purposes. Using the previous example, the forecaster must determine the demands for the various books to be published by the firm. The demand for products that have an external or independent demand must be forecast.

Once the items to be forecast have been selected, a decision must be made about the time period of the forecast. This is done by establishing the forecast horizon, which depends upon many variables. As the horizon is pushed out, confidence in the accuracy of the forecast drops, and the forecasting methodologies become more costly to develop and utilize. Selection of the forecast horizon must consider the product's life cycle, the manufacturing cycle, the firm's ability to gather the necessary production resources, and the cost of developing a forecasting model. The product-life-cycle concept maintains that a product goes through predictable stages: introduction, growth, saturation or maturity, and then decline. Different forecasting models are appropriate depending on the current stage of a product. An industry may experience a manufacturing cycle that requires new models or major new-product introductions at reasonably consistent intervals. Such cycles that exceed annual seasonal patterns will tend to extend the forecast horizon. The forecast horizon must provide adequate visibility into the future for informed decision making as it pertains to plant expansion/contraction and, on a day-to-day basis, sufficient visibility in terms of the purchase of materials and the design of an efficient production plan.

Selecting the Model

Before discussing the actual types of forecasting models, let's consider the criteria for selecting a model. These criteria are listed in exhibit 4-1.

Once decisions concerning each of the criteria have been made, the actual model that best fits this set of decisions may be chosen.

Methods of forecasting. Three general categories of forecasting methods exist—judgmental, intrinsic, and extrinsic. Each differs in terms of the kinds of data utilized and the settings in which each is most effective.

Exhibit 4-1

Forecast Model Selection Criteria

1.   Who will use the forecast, and what are their information needs?

2.   What are the relevance and availability of historical data?

3.   What degree of accuracy is desired?

4.   What time period (horizon) is to be forecast?

5.   How much time is available for making the analysis and forecast?

6.   What is the cost/benefit (value) of the forecast to the company?

Judgmental methods, or qualitative rather than quantitative methods, rely on expert opinions regarding the future. Two examples of judgmental forecasting techniques are the Delphi technique and market-survey techniques.

The Delphi technique utilizes several experts in the area to be forecast. Instead of bringing these experts together and perhaps having their reputations influence one another, the employing firm does not reveal the identities of the experts to each other. The forecasts of these experts are summarized and fed back to each contributor, and their individual revisions are solicited in light of the anonymous views of the group. After several revisions, it is hoped that a consensus can be reached based on the shared expertise. This technique applies where quantitative data are unavailable and judgments of knowledgeable persons can be obtained economically.

Market surveys attempt to measure customer intentions by collecting a sample of opinions. The sample may consist of forecasts by sales personnel, stated intentions of key customers, or a representative consumer panel. Key customers may be especially effective for some industrial suppliers who might have sales concentrated among a small number of accounts. Consumer panels often provide an economical measure of a new consumer-product market. Consumer-opinion surveys, while expensive, are particularly relevant where the firm has no historical experience; for example, it is introducing a new product.

Intrinsic models, or time-series models, extrapolate historical data patterns into the future. The type of intrinsic model used depends on the historical pattern of the forecast variable (e.g., sales units). Time series data can be plotted on graph paper and analyzed for the four basic components of variation. These components are: (1) seasonal, (2) trend, (3) cycle, and (4) the residual, unexplainable component, or random "noise." Graphic illustration of these influences is shown in figure 4-1.

In the fourth, and simplest case, there are no apparent cycles, seasons, or trends. The goal is to smooth out the random noise so that production levels and staffing are not changed in response to transient conditions. Simple models, such as moving averages, weighted average models, and exponential smoothing techniques, apply in this case.

A simple moving average merely sums the data for the most recent months and divides by the number of months. Take a three-month moving average, for example, where the sales were: January, 1,200 units; February, 1,300 units; and March, 1,100 units. The three-month average is 1,200 units, and this would be the forecast for April. Now April has come and gone. April's sales were 1,150 units. To compute the new three-month average, the oldest month is dropped (January's 1,200 units), and the newest demand is added (April's 1,150 units) to get (1,300 + 1,100 + 1,150) ÷ 3 = 1,183.3 or 1,183 units.

A simple weighted average works in much the same way. The three-month moving average really applied a weight of 1/3 to each of the months. In our previous example, we would get the same answer if we added 1/3 × 1,300 plus 1/3 × 1,100 plus 1/3 × 1,150. The advantage of a weighted-average approach is that it allows different emphasis on different pieces of data. For example, we might want to place more importance on last month than the month before. In the case of retail sales, we might want to place more emphasis on Thursday through Saturday sales and less on Monday through Wednesday. The weighted average approach allows this flexibility.

A final variation is called simple exponential smoothing. In this case, we apply a weight, alpha, to the most recent demand. Although alpha can be any value between 0 and 1, typical values are between .1 and .3. The balance of the weight (1-alpha) is placed on the previously exponentially smoothed average. An equivalent approach is to apply the weight, alpha, to the forecast error of the previous period. These two approaches are represented by the following formulas.

$$SF_{t+1} = a(A_t) + (1-a)(SF_t) \text{ or } SF_{t+1} = SF_t + a(A_t - SF_t)$$

Where: SF_t is the smoothed forecast for period t
SF_{t+1} is the smoothed forecast one period in the future
A_t is the actual demand in period t
a is the weighting constant alpha

The three methods—moving average, weighted average, and exponential smoothing—are illustrated in table 4-1. Check to see if you can compute

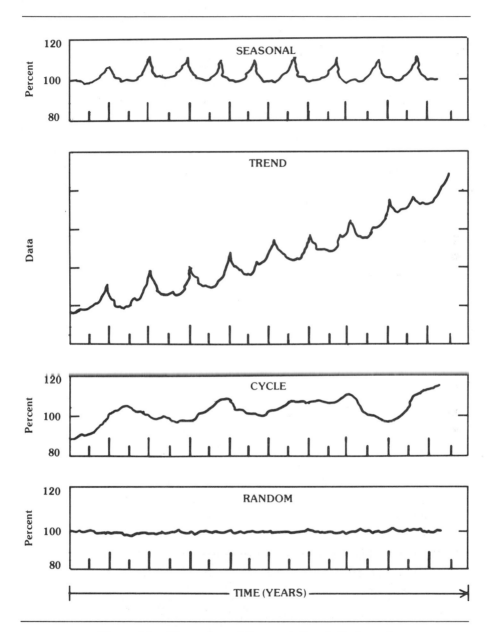

Figure 4-1.   Illustrations of Seasonal, Trend, Cycle, and Random Time-Series Fluctuation Cycles

---

Table 4-1

Methods of Smoothing Random Variations

Month	Demand	3 Month (Moving Average)	3 Month (Weighted Average[a])	Exponential Smoothing[b]
January	1,200	—	—	1,200 (assumed base)
February	1,300	—	—	.1(1,300) + .9(1,200) = 1,210
March	1,100	1,200	1,183.33	.1(1,100) + .9(1,210) = 1,199
April	1,150	1,183.33	1,158.33	.1(1,150) + .9(1,199) = 1,194

[a]Weight1 = 1/6; weight2 = 2/6; weight3 = 3/6

[b]Alpha = .1; The values are the smoothed average for the associated month. The forecast, therefore, for the next month—SF(April) = 1,194—would be the forecast for May.

---

the averages illustrated in table 4-1. Note that the exponential-smoothing model consists of two multiplications and one addition. The moving-average method consists of one addition per month and a division. The weighted-average method consists of one multiplication and one addition per month. The relative efficiency of exponential smoothing is one of its advantages; it also requires the storage of less data.

In cases where a trend is clearly present, the simple moving-average models and exponential smoothing lag behind actual demand and, therefore, do not perform very well. Trends can be handled by making a trend adjustment to the simple exponential-smoothing model. An alternate method is to use linear regression to determine the slope (trend) of the historical data. This method finds the straight line that minimizes the squared errors, as measured by the vertical distance between the historical points and the trend line. Extending this trend line into the future provides a forecast of the expected average sales or other forecast variables. Random variations about these forecast points are to be expected. Also, standard statistical measures are available to evaluate whether or not the trend is statistically significant. If the trend is not significant, then the simple moving average or similar models would be more appropriate. Finally, to be valid, regression models require a significant number of data points and should not be extrapolated into the distant future.

Another matter of concern to the operations manager is the seasonal component. Time-series models handle this by deseasonalizing the data. One approach is the multiplicative model, where a trend line is computed. The trend could be zero, in which case the line represents the average level. Next, each data point is divided by the point on the trend line for the corresponding observed data at that point in time. This tells us what percentage the demand is of the trend line. For example, if the data point is 120 percent of the trend line, then the actual demand can be found by 1.20 × point on the trend line. If we compute these percentages for several years, we can average the percentage for January, February, and so on or for quarter 1, quarter 2, and so on; then these seasonal percentages can be used to forecast the future. First, find the trend point for the future period, and then multiply that value by the seasonal percentage to get the desired forecast. This approach is illustrated in figure 4-2.

The influence of a cyclical factor on time-series models will not be discussed here, but one example would be the demand for Yo-Yos, where the product falls in and out of favor regularly over long time periods.

Extrinsic models attempt to forecast desired variables, such as sales, based on variables outside the system. These models are referred to as causal models because they hypothesize a cause-and-effect relationship between the independent and the dependent (forecasted) variables. The statistical techniques of correlation analysis and regression analysis are the primary means for specifying these relationships. An example of a causal model in forecasting would be a model relating housing permits to lumber sales. By statistical analysis of historical data, it may be found that lumber sales are highly

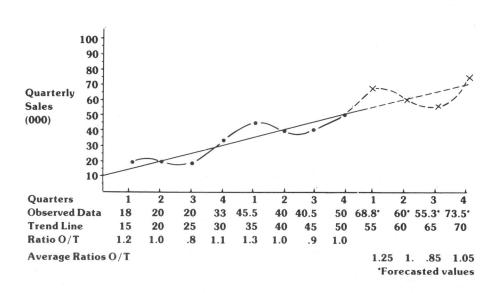

Quarters	1	2	3	4	1	2	3	4	1	2	3	4
Observed Data	18	20	20	33	45.5	40	40.5	50	68.8*	60*	55.3*	73.5*
Trend Line	15	20	25	30	35	40	45	50	55	60	65	70
Ratio O/T	1.2	1.0	.8	1.1	1.3	1.0	.9	1.0				
Average Ratios O/T									1.25	1.	.85	1.05

*Forecasted values

Figure 4-2.   **Multiplicative Model for Trend and Seasonals**

correlated to housing permits and lag behind the permits by two months. Such a model is of great value to the lumber producer, since the number of housing permits issued is easily obtained, and the fact that it provides a two-months' warning of changes in demand is very useful.

Assessing the Model

Now the forecaster must re-examine the model to see if it adequately describes the forecasting situation under the real constraints of time and cost. The model usually is assessed by using historical data to make forecasts for periods in which the level of activity is known. Then, by comparing the model's forecasts with the known outcome, the forecaster can determine the model's predictive ability. If the resulting forecasts are either positively or negatively biased to an unacceptable degree or the magnitude of the errors is excessive, the forecaster must return to the selection step in an effort to reformulate the existing model or choose a different one.

The magnitude of the forecast errors is often measured by the mean absolute deviation (MAD). The MAD is computed by computing the actual demand minus the forecast for a set of historical data. The absolute values (ignore minus signs) of these errors are summed and divided by the number of values to arrive at the average, the MAD. The procedure is easier than computing the standard deviation of the errors and serves the same purpose. Within other constraints, the model that provides a smaller MAD is preferred to one with a larger MAD. Bias in a forecasting model may be evaluated by computing the running sum of the forecast errors (RSFE).

Consider a model that consistently provides forecasts on the low side. The error, actual minus forecast, would be consistently a positive value, and, hence, the RSFE would become a bigger positive value each period. The same would be true if the model consistently provided forecasts on the high-side, except the RSFE would become a bigger negative number. An unbiased forecasting model would tend to overforecast about as often as it would underforecast; therefore, the errors would tend to cancel each other out, resulting in a small RSFE. The MAD and the RSFE are useful measures of a forecasting model's performance.

Applying the Model

Here the acceptable model is put to work in a real forecasting situation. When the model is first put into action, previous forecasting methodologies typically are continued as back-up. By continuing to use the old method, the forecaster has the forecast from the previous technique to use in evaluating the new model.

Evaluating the Model

Because forecasting methodologies are adaptable to computer applications, it is tempting to give the computer total forecasting responsibility. Although safeguards may be built into the computer model to recognize when the forecast exceeds some set of reasonable limits, the human touch is required to make a good evaluation of any model.

Forecast evaluation is a continuing process that requires the forecaster to monitor the validity of each new forecast. Only through judgment can variables external to the model, yet causing fundamental changes in the level of the forecast variable, be recognized.

Planning for Production

Once the future levels of demand for the firm's products have been forecast, the manager must plan the production. At this stage, the manager is concerned with only the broadest level of plant activity rather than with the more detailed scheduling needed to carry out the day-to-day operations. The broad, overall decisions required usually are referred to as aggregate planning, which relates specifically to programming resources over an established time horizon.

Concept of Aggregate Planning

The goal of aggregate planning is to use a representative measure of productive activity and market demand to simplify the selection of a manufacturing strategy that effectively deals with seasonal or cyclical variations in market demand. Management must find a strategy that balances the costs associated with hiring and firing, carrying inventories, having idle facilities, using subcontractors, or losing sales.

Three basic inputs are needed to make aggregate planning decisions. The first is the development of a single, overall measure of production. This is relatively easy for a one-product firm. Firms that produce many and diverse products, however, need a measure that represents the product mix and manufacturing processes, so that labor and equipment capabilities will be fairly represented. For example, cases of soft drink for a bottling plant, tons for a steel mill, cars for an automobile assembly plant, or equivalent machine-hours for a job shop may serve as representative measures. The second requirement is forecasting the selected measure of output with some reasonable degree of accuracy over the planning period. These forecasts represent the market's demands on the firm's capacity in each of the planning periods. The final input needed is a determination of the costs associated with each of the resources that will be combined in a strategy for meeting the market demand.

Manufacturing strategies fall along a continuum from level production (the same number of units each period) to a variable-production approach (match the units produced to the number the market demands). The level-production plan leads to storing inventories during slow sales periods so the product will be available when the demand increases above the firm's steady production rate. This approach utilizes plant and equipment effectively and maintains a stable work force at the expense of warehouse space, dollars in stocks, and related costs of inventory. In some cases, the firm can "store" the market demand by a back-order strategy; this method makes the customer wait longer during the peak season than in the off season. If the market permits this strategy, the firm can produce at a steady rate and still not require excessive inventories. An organization may not have the option of an inventory strategy—for example, those service industries or firms that provide a highly perishable product. In this case, varying production rates can be achieved by hiring and firing, overtime, or subcontracting the excess demand to other firms. In between these two extreme strategies are any number of combinations using some level of inventory, some overtime and hiring or firing, some back ordering, and some level of subcontracting. Finding a good balance is the challenge.

Making the Aggregate Plan

The aggregate plan should establish the employment levels, production rates, inventory levels, back-order levels, and magnitude of subcontracting for each period over the planning horizon. The various techniques for solving aggregate planning problems involve varying levels of cost and sophistication in their development and implementation. These techniques include graphing, mathematical programming, heuristic decision rules, search techniques, and simulation.

Graphical methods plot the chosen aggregate measure (e.g., tons, units, or hours) against production periods over the planning horizon. Cumulative data are plotted, providing a year-to-date graph of market demand. On this same graph, various production plans can be tested against constraints imposed by management. Such constraints might include upper limits on inventory, hiring/firing, or back orders. A cumulative graph of production provides the year-to-date available units for sale at any given time over the planning horizon. An inventory balance exists whenever the point on the cumulative production graph is above the corresponding point (same time in the year) on the cumulative market-demand graph. Similarly, if, at a specified point, the cumulative market graph is above the cumulative production graph, this is a back-order situation, since, year-to-date, fewer units have been supplied by production than desired by the market. Changes in the slope of the cumulative production graph signify changes in the production rate and imply changes in the labor force and possibly hiring and firing. This graphical trial-and-error technique does not guarantee an optimum solution, but it does provide a quick and visual method of evaluating possible alternative manu-facturing plans.

Mathematical programming methods provide optimal solutions within the constraints and assumptions of the models. Linear, quadratic, and goal-programming algorithms are some of the techniques available to optimize a cost or profit objective function subject to one or more resource contraints—for example, inventory less than or equal to $1,000,000. While more so-phisticated, these methods are more costly to develop and utilize than the graphical approach.

Heuristic decision rules require systematic evaluations of various cost functions at a selected number of trial points. An attempt is made to minimize the cost function, but heuristic methods do not test for minimums over the entire range of the function. It is possible, therefore, to state only that the best minimum has been found, based on that set of decision rules. These models may be less costly to construct and implement than programming models, but they do not assure an optimal solution.

Heuristic decision rules or programming models may be designed into search techniques that will evaluate an objective function at many different points, as variables are manipulated. Such models can deal with some of the weaknesses of the heuristic and programming models but not without sig-nificant costs of development and computer time. Optimal solutions are still not guaranteed.

Regardless of the method used, an aggregate plan is the outcome of the analysis. This aggregate plan is stated in the selected broad measure of production and is not suitable for the detailed scheduling of labor and work centers. Translating the aggregate plan into the manufacture of specific prod-ucts on specific dates is the task of master scheduling.

Scheduling Production

Once the aggregate plan has been developed based on the planned resources available and the market demand, the disaggregating process begins and leads to the specific production plan. The goal is to establish a realistic master production schedule from which detailed shop loadings and job order se-quences are derived. The disaggregation process and its trial-and-error nature are illustrated in figure 4-3.

The Master Schedule

The master schedule states the desired quantities to be produced by end product or product group. It also indicates when the "end items" are to be available. The guiding principle for setting a master schedule is to make it realistic. A common error in practice is to schedule excessive production quantities, even though it is not remotely possible to achieve the schedule.

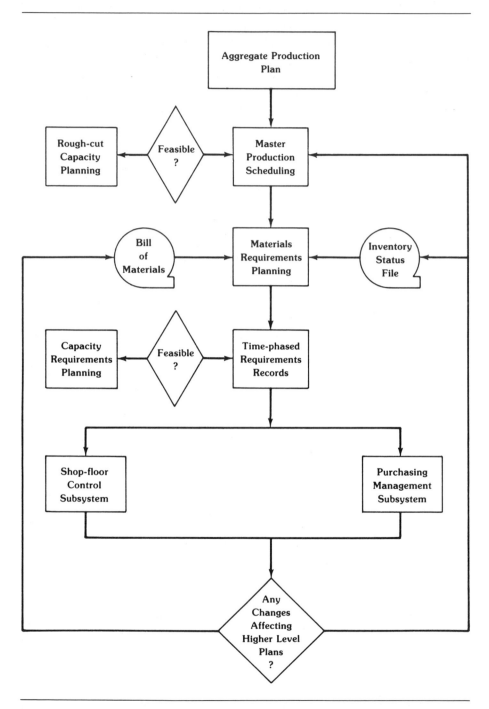

Figure 4-3.   The Detailed Schedule

Difficulties can occur when the product mix in the aggregate plan is such that the organization cannot adhere to the aggregate plan without expensive strategies, such as excessive hiring and firing or a massive inventory buildup during slack periods. The assignment of specific products to be made in specific time periods brings with it the need to check the demands on the productive resources of the organization. This checking generally focuses on key resources that might bottleneck the flow of work through the organization. The consequences of a specific master schedule can be evaluated by "exploding" the schedule into the components and materials that comprise the end products; this exploding process is one function of material requirements planning (MRP). The logic of MRP is covered in detail in chapter 6. For now, it is sufficient to realize that MRP will indicate how many units of subassemblies, parts, and raw materials will be needed and when. This information by itself, however, does not answer the question: Is the master schedule realistic and feasible? The units must be translated into machines and labor hours. This process is part of capacity requirements planning (CRP).

Capacity Requirements Planning

CRP is concerned with the loading of specific jobs onto various work centers for specific periods of time. By combining MRP data on the timing of units needed with standard data on manufacturing processes, one can identify the machine hours and labor hours required by a work center to meet the master schedule. There are two general approaches to loading: (1) infinite loading and (2) finite loading.

Infinite loading assumes that each work center has sufficient capacity to produce whatever it is assigned, using standard manufacturing processes. This approach has the main advantage of being simple. When a plant has more-than-ample capacity, it may be valid to assume that no resource will be strained to capacity. Here infinite loading is both simple and effective. But, regardless of the short-term validity of infinite loading, it is useful for long-term capacity planning. Because infinite loading assumes use of the primary method of manufacturing and no limit in capacity, it gives a good picture of what capacity the plant should have in the future.

Finite loading does not assume that enough capacity will be available in all work centers and does not restrict itself to the primary method of manufacture. The elimination of these two assumptions makes the analysis much more complicated and time consuming. In essence, when a bottleneck is encountered, the load is shifted to secondary methods in work centers with available capacity, or the load is shifted to different time slots. Allowing loads to be shifted in these ways opens up for consideration thousands of possible schedules. The large number of alternatives makes this problem impressive even when large-scale computers are available. Techniques such as linear programming, simulation, and heuristic rules have been applied to solve this problem. The advantage of finite loading is that it indicates what can be produced in the short term—that is, what is realistic given current conditions.

Sequencing Jobs

The loading of work centers for a block of time does not specify the order in which the individual jobs are to be processed. Often this sequencing is left to the foreman, or a central planning group may specify the sequence based on sophisticated computerized analysis. In either event, some of the common goals are: (1) maximum flow through the shop, (2) minimum number of late orders, (3) minimum average lateness, (4) minimum variance from due dates, and (5) minimum cost.

One way to sequence jobs is to use a priority rule. There are many such rules, each with its own unique performance characteristics. One popular priority rule is the shortest-operation-time job first (SOT). This rule is effective with respect to minimizing the average flow time through the shop. Its major weakness is that long jobs continually may be "bumped" to last and thereby delayed excessively. Since long jobs may be the most important jobs, it might make sense to use another priority rule, one called longest-operation-time first (LOT). The performance characteristics of this rule are the opposite of SOT. The choice of a priority rule depends upon what is important to the organization; obviously, no rule will achieve all the possible desirable goals.

Other common priority rules are summarized in exhibit 4-2. First come, first served (FCFS) is an easily defended rule as far as customers are concerned. The various slack rules consider how much time there is between a reference time, for example, time of arrival at a work center, and the due date. Some rules divide this by a measure of the amount of work that still remains to be done, such as the remaining processing time or the number of operations remaining. Such ratios give a measure of urgency for each job.

Development of Detailed Schedules

When all the aforementioned decisions and revisions have been made, detailed schedules finally will be prepared. Detailed schedules take the job and flow sequences established at the last stage and overlay them on a time scale, which is divided into periods appropriate for the manufacturing setting, extending over the entire planning period. Job shops may require daily scales, while an assembly line might use weekly or longer time frames. Gantt charts are particularly useful in blocking out plans and providing quick and easy visual presentation. Figure 4-4 illustrates a set of work orders scheduled using the common Gantt chart symbols. By updating progress on the chart, one can see at a glance the jobs that are behind schedule, on time, and ahead of schedule, as well as the jobs coming up in the near future. Such a chart

Exhibit 4-2

Job Shop Priority Scheduling Rules

FCFS — First come, first served—priority based upon time of arrival at the work center or place in line.

SOT — Shortest operation time—process the quickest jobs first. This rule maximizes mean flow rate but tends to delay excessively the important large jobs.

SS — Static slack—compute the difference between the time of arrival and the due date. Process first those with the smallest difference (slack). This rule is called static because it does not change as time passes; the arrival date and due date are fixed.

SS/PT — Static slack per remaining processing time—do those jobs in which you have the most work to do in the least time.

SS/RO — Static slack per remaining number of operations—similar to SS/PT, but emphasis is on the number of remaining tasks, not the time required by these tasks. This is relevant when the time between jobs is more significant than the processing time itself.

FISFS — First in system, first served—this differs from FCFS, where the priority can change at each work center. Example: air travelers flying standby have priority based on when they started the journey, not necessarily when they arrived at an intermediate stop.

LCFS — Last come, first served—this is a convenience rule that means do the job on top of the stack first.

DS
DS/PT
DS/RO — These are dynamic versions of the static slack rules. In these cases, the slack changes as time passes; it is due date minus the current date.

Critical Ratio — This is the ratio of time remaining to work time remaining. This is a popular dynamic rule in which a job with a ratio > 1 is ahead of schedule, ratio of 1 is on schedule, and a ratio < 1 needs to be expedited.

facilitates the coordination of setups, maintenance, and scheduling of labor crews.

After scheduling conflicts have been resolved, specific start and finish dates are assigned to jobs. These start and finish dates may be set by working

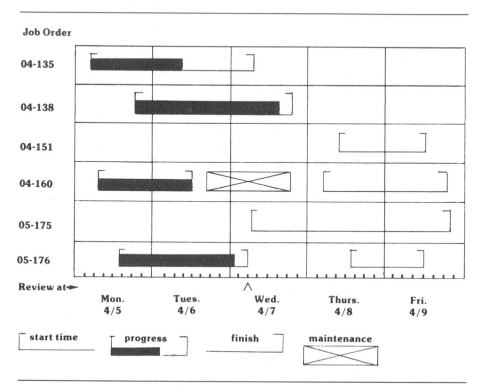

Figure 4-4.   Gantt Chart

back from the due date on a job (backward scheduling) or by starting a job as early as possible (forward scheduling.) Backward scheduling reduces inventory and maintains flexibility on schedule changes as long as possible, at the risk of having more late jobs than with a forward-scheduling approach. In either case, when the start date is reached on a dispatch list, work orders are released to the manufacturing facility, and processing commences.

Progress Control/Shop Floor Control

Progress control, the final stage in the scheduling process, involves constantly monitoring the jobs as they pass through the facility in an attempt to detect and to resolve problems that may arise. One method of detecting problems or bottlenecks in the flow of jobs is via input/output control charts. I/O control charts monitor planned work inputs and outputs against actual inputs and outputs by work center. If backlogs arise, the I/O table focuses attention on the work center causing the problem. Another means of monitoring and sequencing jobs through a shop is called Kanban. This is a simple card-oriented, manual system made popular by the Japanese as part of the just-in-time approach to shop floor control. The cards are used to authorize production and transfer of materials between operations. Control of the number of cards controls the flow of materials and highlights bottlenecks.

Identified bottlenecks can be managed in several ways. Expediting can get a late job back on schedule by reducing the time spent waiting for jobs ahead of it. This works when some of the jobs ahead of the late one can be delayed. Lot splitting and lap scheduling speed a job through a facility by reducing the delay in waiting for a large production run to complete one task before starting the next task. Alternate routings, using other machines or processes, can temporarily deal with a bottleneck and keep jobs on schedule. If the schedule cannot be maintained, then feedback to the scheduling process may lead to a revised master schedule.

Managing the shop floor requires constant revision of plans. This necessitates accurate and current feedback data on the status of in-process jobs.

PERT/CPM

The program evaluation and review technique (PERT) and the critical path method (CPM) are widely recognized and successfully applied techniques that require special attention. These similar methodologies belong to a special set of operations-research techniques known as network models. They are particularly applicable to the management of unique projects that have a broad scope.

PERT and CPM are so similar that it is unnecessary to attempt to distinguish one from the other. PERT originally was developed by the U.S. Navy Special Projects Office and Lockheed Aircraft Corporation in cooperation with the consulting firm of Booz, Allen, and Hamilton. It was introduced in 1958 in an effort to reduce the original time forecast for the development of the Polaris ballistic missile and is credited with reducing the time span by several years. CPM was developed in 1957 to help with the scheduling of maintenance in chemical plants. Next to PERT, CPM is the second most widely used system for planning and controlling large projects. Both techniques have been applied to such projects as start-ups and shutdowns of production facilities; installations of major new equipment, such as computer systems and assembly lines; construction of subdivisions, shopping centers, skyscrapers, dams, and power stations; and virtually all government development contracts.

As a planning tool, PERT allows the manager to plan a project well in advance and estimate its expected completion time and date. This early planning identifies possible bottlenecks and indicates which activities may require modification. For controlling the project, PERT permits the manager to compare the actual and planned progress of each activity. This procedure identifies those activities that are behind schedule and that ultimately may delay the overall project completion date.

PERT Network Analysis

The PERT analysis proceeds chronologically through the following steps:

1. Identification of activities required by the project
2. Identification of the precedence relationships among the activities (i.e., which activities must be completed before others can begin)
3. Determination of the expected time requirements for each activity
4. Development of the network diagram of activities (arrows) and events or nodes (circles)
5. Determination of the earliest and latest feasible event times (an event is the beginning or end of an activity)
6. Identification of the critical path

Steps 1 through 3 require extensive data gathering from people knowledgeable about the various activities of the project. Because their expert opinions form the basis for the PERT analysis, they represent a critical input to the planning. It is important to solicit the full and honest cooperation of these people, who, in many cases, will be the same people responsible for the successful implementation of the project plans.

Network diagramming.   The network must relate the activities so that each arrow representing an activity does not begin before all necessary preceding requirements have been completed. Furthermore, each activity should be described uniquely by its starting and ending event nodes. The latter requirement leads to the use of "dummy" activities, those that require zero time but permit the unique identification of activities. The network representing a simplified equipment installation is developed in table 4-2 and figure 4-5.

In table 4-2, three times are provided by the experts: optimistic, most likely, and pessimistic. Since the actual distribution of times may be skewed instead of symmetrical, it may be difficult for the experts to estimate directly the mean (expected) time. In PERT, the expected time is computed as a weighted average of the three time estimates. Traditionally, the optimistic and pessimistic estimates are given a weight of one, and the most likely is given a weight of four. The computed expected time is the estimate used in evaluating the PERT network.

The precedence requirements in table 4-2 resulted in the network in figure 4-5. Check the network to assure yourself that you understand how the precedence relationships are incorporated into the diagram. For example, notice that activities C and E cannot begin until activity B has been completed. Event 3 marks the completion of activity B and the beginning of activities C

Table 4-2

PERT Data on Activities: Precedence and Time Estimates

ACTIVITY		TIME	TIME	TIME	TIME	Precedence Relation-
Code	Description	Optimistic	Most Likely	Pessimistic	Expected*	ships
A	Acquire Equipment	20 days	25 days	36 days	26 days	None
B	Clear Floor Space	2	5	8	5	None
C	Mark Floor Location	1	3	11	4	B
D	Inspect Equipment	1	1	7	2	A
E	Store Installation Materials	1	1	1	1	B
F	Install Equipment	5	10	27	12	C,D,E
G	Test & Debug Equip.	3	7	23	9	F

*Expected Time $= \dfrac{t(optimistic) + 4 \times t(most\ likely) + t(pessimistic)}{6}$

and E. The dummy activity is required to uniquely identify activity E; otherwise, both activities C and E would begin at node 3 and end at node 5.

Determining earliest and latest event times.   The earliest possible event times are computed first in what is termed the "forward pass." Starting with the first node, we set the earliest event time to zero. We call this the early start time (ES). To compute the ES for node 2, we add the time from node 1 to 2, or 26 days to the ES(1), which was 0. Next we compute ES(3) = 0 + 5, or 5 days. This says that day 5 is the earliest we can expect to have progressed as far as event 3. Similarly, ES(4) = ES(3) + expected time for activity E, which numerically means that ES(4) = 5 + 1 or 6 days from the start date. Event 5 is more complicated because there are several paths leading to that node: path 1-2-5, path 1-3-5, and path 1-3-4-5. We must find the longest of these three paths since all the associated activities must be completed before event 5 is reached and activity F can begin. To find the longest path, we merely have to check each of the arrows (activities) leading into node 5. Therefore, for activity D, we compute ES(5) = ES(2) + T(D) = 26 + 2 = 28. For activity C, ES(5) = ES(3) + T(C) = 5 + 4 = 9. For the dummy, ES(5) = ES(4) + T(dummy) = 6 + 0 = 6. We identify the largest of the three, 28 days, and this becomes the ES(5). ES(6) and ES(7) are computed in the same manner and result in ES(7) of 49 days, which is the earliest we can expect to complete the installation.

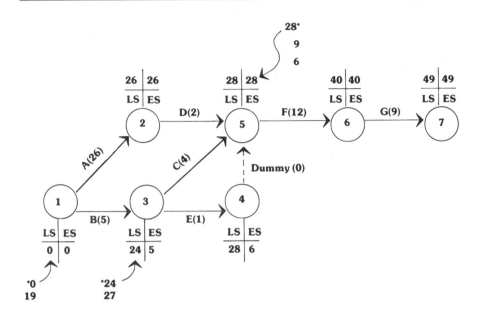

Figure 4-5.   PERT Network

* Indicates the selected values when more than one path is relevant to the computation of LS (latest start time) or ES (earliest start time).

The next step is the "backward pass," and it follows a similar logic. We begin with the last node, event 7. Since 49 days is the earliest we can complete the project, we set the latest time for this event equal to 49 days. We will call this LS(7). Now we wish to compute the latest time for each of the preceding events that will not delay our completion on day 49. Working backwards, if we need to reach node 7 on day 49, when do we need to be at node 6? Clearly we need to be at node 6 no later than on the 40th day. Therefore, the latest start (LS) of activity 6 must be 40. For node 5, we compute LS(5) = LS(6) − T(F) = 40 − 12 = 28. LS(4) = LS(5) − T(dummy) = 28 − 0 = 28. Node 3 is more complex (similar to node 5 in the forward pass). Node 3 has two arrows that trace backwards to it; therefore, we need to evaluate two paths. The two computations are: LS(3) = LS(5) − T(C) = 28 − 4 = 24 and LS(3) = LS(4) − T(E) = 28 − 1 = 27. In the backward pass, we must choose the smaller of the two, thus LS(3) = 24. Logically, consider what the consequences would be if event 3 were not achieved until sometime after the 24th day. It would delay the completion of the project due to the time required by activities C,F, and G. Latest start times for nodes 2 and 1 are computed the same way. LS(1) will be 0 unless you have made an arithmetic error.

The critical path.   The critical path consists of those activities that determine the earliest completion of the project. The critical activities must be completed on time or the project will be delayed; in other words, there is zero "slack" for these activities. Zero slack is present when the LS − ES = 0 for a node. Therefore, activities that connect nodes with zero slack are candidates for the critical path. In figure 4-5 nodes 1,2,5,6, and 7 have zero slack. The associated activities are A, D, F, and G. In this case, there is no ambiguity: these are the critical activities. Consider an additional activity— H. Activity H is to fly in an installation expert who must be there before installation, but there are no required preceding activities. Therefore, activity H, which takes 2 days, connects node 1 and node 5. Here we have an example in which activity H connects two nodes with zero slack but is not a critical activity. Do you see why it is not critical?

Now that we have an estimate of our earliest completion date and have identified the critical activities, we can consider whether or not we need to finish sooner and, if so, which activities we must expedite. If management requires the new equipment in operation 40 days from now, then we will focus our speed-up efforts on activities A, D, F, and G. Since we have a great deal of slack in activities B (24 − 5 = 19 days), C (28 − 9 = 19 days), and E (28 − 6 = 22 days), we need not be very concerned that our expediting will lead to another path becoming critical. In other projects, however, we must be concerned about near critical paths—that is, those with little slack.

Using the PERT Network

The PERT network is not an inflexible, unalterable schedule. It is a dynamic tool that allows new networks to be formulated as changes occur in the schedule due to a lack of resources or in order to utilize available resources more effectively. The planner who understands this flexibility may find that rearranging activities or moving resources to the most critical areas can significantly reduce the total time required.

Materials Requirements Planning

Materials requirements planning (MRP) is a process that translates the master schedule into time-phased materials requirements. MRP, which is discussed in depth in chapter 6, is an important planning tool. Figure 4-6 illustrates the variety of information that is integrated in an MRP system. The forecasting information enters through the master schedule. Inventory strategies and status enter by way of the inventory status file. New-product designs and engineering changes enter the system through the bill of materials file. MRP combines the information from the three data bases and indicates how many of each item in our production mix should be purchased or produced and when.

The planning significance of MRP is that it provides a basis for capacity requirements planning, as discussed earlier in this chapter. It provides information on the number of labor and machine hours required and when they are required. This permits the identification of overloads of specific categories of either labor or machines. As a scheduling tool, MRP identifies inconsistencies in current plans, such as violation of normal lead-time requirements. In such cases, MRP will indicate that certain materials, parts, assemblies, or final products are planned for time slots that cannot be achieved by normal procedures. This alerts management either to (1) expedite, (2) subcontract, or (3) reschedule.

MRP is of further use in the planning of engineering changes and inventory levels. It clearly projects the status of production plans and inventory over a planning horizon, and serves as a valuable management tool for phasing in engineering changes and thus minimizing waste due to obsolete inventories. In addition to managing the introduction of changes, MRP provides a basis

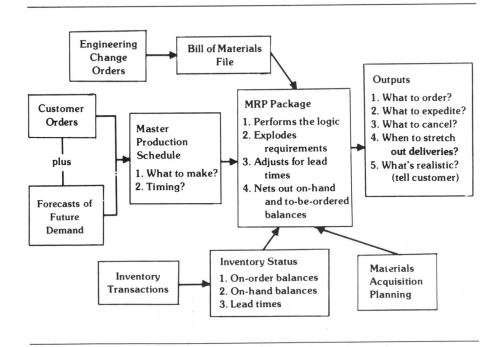

Figure 4-6. The MRP System

for projecting inventory investment over the planning horizon, which is valuable to the financial planners as well as those managing the use of warehouse space and the purchase of materials.

Although MRP is an important advance in the management of operations, it suffers the weakness of any computerized management system—that is, the problem of garbage in, garbage out. Therefore, users of MRP must be particularly diligent in keeping accurate inventory records, up-to-date bills of materials, and realistic master schedules. Otherwise, MRP deteriorates into a mechanized error generator. This challenge has required extensive re education and significant procedural changes in many companies.

References

Buffa, Elwcod S., and Miller, Jeffrey. *Production and Inventory Systems.* Homewood, IL: Richard D. Irwin, 1979.

Chase, Richard B., and Aquilano, Nicholas J. *Production and Operations Management.* 4th ed. Homewood, IL: Richard D. Irwin, 1985.

Makridakis, Spyros, and Wheelwright, Steven C. *Forecasting Methods and Applications.* Santa Barbara, CA: John Wiley & Sons, 1978.

Meredith, Jack R., and Mantel, Samuel J., Jr. *Project Management.* New York: John Wiley & Sons, 1985.

Silver, Edward A., and Peterson, Rein. *Decision Systems for Inventory Management and Production Planning.* New York: John Wiley & Sons, 1985.

Vollmann, Thomas E.; Berry, William L.; and Whybark, D. Clay. *Manufacturing Planning and Control Systems.* Homewood, IL: Richard D. Irwin, 1984.

Discussion Questions

1. What are the five basic steps in the forecasting process?

2. How does external, market demand differ from internal, dependent demand? Why are the differences important?

3. Identify three general types of forecasting models, and discuss how they differ.

4. Identify four influences (components) that may be found in a set of time series data. Why are they important to a forecaster?

5. How can you measure whether or not your forecasting model is doing a good job?

6. What is the manager attempting to accomplish with aggregate planning?

7. What trade-offs are the focus of the aggregate planning process?

8. Discuss this statement: "Capacity requirements planning validates the master production schedule."

9. What types of problems justify the use of PERT? Why is PERT particularly helpful in these situations?

10. How do split lots and lap scheduling speed some jobs through the shop?

Problems

1. Given the following historical data, use simple exponential smoothing to forecast sales for July. Use an alpha of .1 and assume the smoothed forecast for January was 1,100 units.

t	Month	Actual Demand (A_t)	Smoothed Forecast (SF_t)
1	January	1150	1,100 (initial smoothed forecast)
2	February	1075	_____
3	March	1230	_____
4	April	1020	_____
5	May	1185	_____
6	June	1045	_____
7	July		_____

2. Given the data on the four jobs A, B, C, and D, sequence them into work center 1 based on—SOT, SS, and critical ratio priority rules. Which rule gives the smallest average lateness per four jobs? Per late jobs only? Today is Tuesday. The current day is available to schedule, as are the days when a job is received. Work is scheduled Monday through Friday.

Job	Total Work per Job	Work Remaining on Each Job	Date Received	Due Date
A	3 Days	2 Days	Yesterday	Friday
B	2 Days	2 Days	Today	Wednesday
C	5 Days	4 Days	Last Thur.	Next Tuesday
D	1 Day	1 Day	Today	Next Monday

3. Compute the following for the given PERT diagram (assuming that the
    activity times provided are the expected times):
    a.   The early start times for each event (ES)
    b.   The late start times for each event (LS)
    c.   The critical path
    d.   The slack times for each event

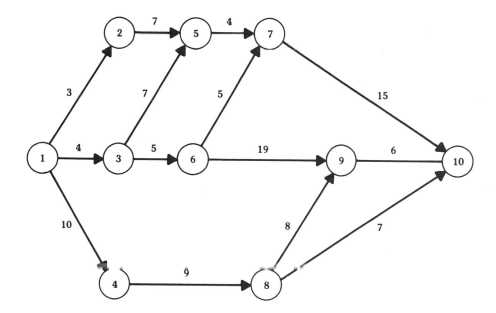

Chapter 5

Purchasing/Materials Management

Any organization, whether it is a bank, computer manufacturer, hospital, airline, governmental agency, or automobile producer, must have a continuous flow of materials, supplies, and services to support operations. The supply of these items typically is handled through the organization's purchasing department, which has the managerial responsibility of *providing, from outside vendors or suppliers, a smooth supply of materials, supplies, and services to support operations.*

Prior to World War I, most firms regarded the purchasing function primarily as a clerical activity. During both World War I (1915-1918) and World War II (1939-1945), however, the success of a firm was not dependent on what it could sell, since demand was almost unlimited. Instead, the ability to obtain, from vendors, the raw materials, supplies, and services needed to keep the production process operating was the key determinant of organization success. Because attention was given to the organization, policies, and procedures of the purchasing function, it emerged as a recognized managerial activity. During the 1950s and 1960s, purchasing continued to gain stature as the techniques for performing the function became more refined and as the supply of people trained and competent to make sound purchasing decisions increased. Many companies elevated the chief purchasing officer to top management status, with a title such as vice-president of purchasing, director of materials, or vice-president of purchasing and supply.

In the early 1970s, firms faced two vexing problems: an international shortage of almost all the basic raw materials needed to support operations and the fastest rate of price increases since the end of World War II. The Middle East oil embargo during the summer of 1973 intensified both the shortages and the price escalation. These developments put the spotlight directly on companies' purchasing departments, for their performance in obtaining needed items from vendors, at realistic prices, spelled the difference between success and failure. This emphasized again to top management the crucial role played by purchasing. Although the shortages lessened from 1974 to 1975, due to the worldwide recession, and the inflationary trend moderated in 1982, due to stringent government monetary and fiscal actions and a worldwide glut of crude oil, companies now recognize the importance of a capable, efficient purchasing function. Additionally, the purchasing department plays a key role in combating inflationary pressures by resisting unwarranted price increases.

As a result of this recognition of the impact of purchasing decisions on the long-term success of a firm (assuring a reliable supply of needed materials at a reasonable cost), many firms now are emphasizing strategic material planning. This activity attempts to forecast the long-term (five to twenty years) demand, supply, and price of those key raw materials needed to operate the firm based upon a variety of assumptions about the worldwide economic and political environment. If future problems in demand, supply, and price can be spotted now, the firm can take action by, for example, substitution, backward vertical integration, or product line reduction to alleviate the difficulty before a crisis occurs.

Objectives of Purchasing/Materials Management

Basically, the function of the purchasing department is to obtain the *right materials* (meeting quality requirements), in the *right quantity*, for delivery at the *right time* and *right place*, from the *right source* (a reliable vendor who will meet commitments in a timely fashion), with the *right service* (both before and after the sale), and at the *right price*. The purchasing decision maker might be likened to a juggler attempting to keep several balls in the air at the same time: the purchaser must achieve several goals—the seven "rights" just listed—simultaneously. It is not efficient to buy at the lowest price, if the goods delivered are unsatisfactory from a quality/performance standpoint or if they arrive two weeks behind schedule, causing a production slowdown or shutdown. The right price may be one that is much *higher* than normal if the item is needed immediately, preventing the buyer from adhering to the normal lead time. The purchasing decision maker attempts to balance out the often conflicting objectives and makes trade-offs to obtain the optimum mix of these seven "rights."

A more specific statement of the overall goals of purchasing would include the following eight items. Purchasing should:

1. Provide an uninterrupted flow of materials, supplies, and services required to operate the organization. Stock-outs (interruptions in supply) of raw materials and production parts would shut down an operation

and be extremely costly in terms of lost production, escalation of operating costs due to fixed costs, and inability to satisfy delivery promises to customers. For example, an automobile producer cannot complete the car without purchased tires; an airline cannot keep its planes flying without purchased fuel; and a hospital cannot perform surgery without purchased IV (intravenous) solutions.

2. Minimize inventory investment and loss. One way to assure an uninterrupted material flow is to keep large inventory banks. But inventory assets require using capital that could be invested elsewhere; the cost of carrying inventory may be 24 to 36 percent of value per year. If purchasing can support operations with an inventory investment of $10 million instead of $20 million, at an annual inventory carrying cost of 30 percent, the $10 milion reduction in inventory represents a saving of $3 million.

3. Maintain adequate quality standards. To produce the desired product or service, a certain quality level is required for each material input. Otherwise, the end product or service will not meet expectations or will result in higher-than-acceptable production costs. For example, if poor-quality carbon paper is supplied to secretarial personnel, the appearance of the final typed product will not be satisfactory, and much typing will have to be redone.

4. Find or develop competent vendors. In the final analysis, the success of the purchasing department depends on its skill in locating or developing vendors, analyzing vendor capabilities, and then selecting the appropriate vendor. Only if vendors who are both responsive and responsible are selected will the firm obtain the items it needs at the lowest ultimate cost. For example, if a complex computer system is purchased from a vendor who later goes out of business and is not able to perform the long-term maintenance, modification, and updating of the system, the initial favorable price turns out to be extremely high because of the vendor's inability to make good on the original commitment.

5. Standardize, where possible, the items bought. From an overall company viewpoint, the best item possible for the intended application should be bought. If purchasing can buy a quantity of one item to do the job that two or three different items previously did, the organization may gain efficiency advantages through a lower initial price resulting from a quantity discount, lower total inventory investment (without lowering service levels), reduced personnel training and maintenance costs in the use of equipment, and increased competition.

6. Maintain the organization's competitive position. An organization will be competitive only if it can control purchasing costs to protect profit margins; these costs are the largest single element in the operation of many

organizations. Additionally, product design and manufacturing methods must change to keep pace with changing technology and production environments; the purchasing department can inform product design and manufacturing engineering about new products available and changes likely to occur in production technology. Finally, the purchasing department is responsible for assuring the smooth flow of materials necessary to produce products and provide services as required to meet delivery commitments to customers; in the long run, the success of any organization depends upon its ability to create and maintain a customer.

7. Achieve harmonious, productive working relationships with other departments within the organization. Purchasing actions cannot be effectively accomplished solely by the efforts of the purchasing department; cooperation with several other departments and individuals within the firm is vital to success. For example, the using departments and production control must provide timely information on material requirements if purchasing is to have sufficient lead time to locate competent vendors and make advantageous purchase agreements. Engineering and production must be willing to consider the possible economic advantages of using substitute materials and different vendors. Purchasing must work closely with quality control in determining inspection procedures for incoming materials, in communicating to vendors the changes needed if quality problems are found, and assisting in evaluating the performance of current vendors. To take advantage of payment discounts and maintain good, long-term vendor relations, accounting must pay vendors on time. If there is a problem with the flow of information concerning payment to vendors, purchasing must correct the problem; the vendor deals directly with purchasing, not with accounting, receiving, or incoming inspection, and expects to be paid on schedule.

8. Accomplish the purchasing objectives at the lowest possible level of administrative costs. It takes resources to operate the purchasing department—salaries, telephone and postage expenses, supplies, travel costs, and accompanying overhead. If purchasing procedures are not efficient, purchasing administrative costs will be excessive. Because the objectives of purchasing should be achieved as efficiently and economically as possible, the purchasing manager continually must review the operation to assure that it is cost-effective. If the firm is not realizing its purchasing objectives due to inadequate analysis and planning, perhaps additional personnel are needed. But the firm should be continually alert to possible improvements in purchasing methods, procedures, and techniques. Perhaps unneeded steps in processing purchasing paperwork could be eliminated; perhaps the computer could be used to make the storage and recall of necessary purchasing data more efficient.

Importance of the Purchasing Function

The key objectives of any organization are to provide a good or service needed by a customer and to do so effectively and efficiently in order to return adequate long-term rewards (profits) to the owners. The purchasing function plays an important role in achieving these key objectives.

Total Dollars Involved

Purchasing is the largest single dollar control area with which most managements must deal. Obviously, the percent of the sales or income dollar paid out to vendors will vary greatly from industry to industry. For example, in a hospital or bank, purchasing dollars as a percent of operating income will be less than 25 percent since these industries are labor- rather than material-intensive. But in the manufacturing sector, material dollars typically account for well over half the sales dollar. When an automobile producer sells a new car to a dealer for $10,000, it already has spent more than $5,000 (over 50 percent) to buy the steel, tires, glass, paint, fabric, aluminum, copper, and electronic components necessary to build that car. When a soft-drink producer sells $1,000 of packaged beverages to the supermarket, close to $750 already has been paid to vendors for the liquid sugar, carbonation, flavoring, bottles, caps, and cardboard containers necessary to produce the end product.

Table 5-1, which uses data collected by the U.S. Bureau of the Census for its *Annual Survey of Manufacturers*, presents aggregate data for the entire U.S. manufacturing sector, broken down by type of industry. These figures show that, in the average manufacturing firm, materials account for 59 percent of the sales dollar; if expenditures for capital equipment are included, the figure goes up to 63 percent. This is about one-and-a-half times the remaining 37 percent available to pay salaries, wages, other operating expenses, taxes, and dividends. In 1981, the 63 percent total purchase/sales ratio was exactly three times the 21 percent spent for all wages, salaries, and fringe benefits.

The material/sales ratio varies dramatically among industries. For example, in standard industrial classification (SIC) 38, "Instruments and Related Products," it is only 36 percent; but this industry includes firms making such items as the auto-pilot used on large commercial aircraft, which requires a higher percentage of engineering, quality control, and direct assembly labor. On the other hand, in SIC 20, "Food and Kindred Products," the material/sales ratio is 70 percent, almost twice as large. This category includes commercial bread bakeries and beverage producers whose production process is material-intensive and requires a minimum amount of labor cost due to highly mechanized/automated manufacturing processes.

Table 5-1 shows that the average material/sales ratio in manufacturing has moved up from 53 percent in 1971 to 59 percent in 1981 because manufacturing processes have become more material- and less labor-intensive.

Table 5-1

Cost of Materials—Value of Industry Shipments Ratios for Manufacturing Firms, 1981

Standard Industrial Code	Industry	Cost of Materials (Millions)*	Capital Expenditures, New (Millions)†	Total Material and Capital Expenditures (Millions)	Value of Industry Shipments (Millions)‡	Material Sales Ratio	Total Purchase Sales Ratio
20	Food and kindred products	191,594	6,012	197,606	272,139	70	73
21	Tobacco products	6,690	726	7,416	13,129	51	56
22	Textile mill products	31,061	1,724	32,785	50,262	62	65
23	Apparel and other textile products	24,657	646	25,303	49,822	49	51
24	Lumber and wood products	29,473	1,781	31,254	46,807	63	67
25	Furniture and fixtures	11,426	573	11,999	23,865	48	50
26	Paper and allied products	48,312	4,655	52,967	80,233	60	66
27	Printing and publishing	28,131	3,075	31,206	77,260	36	40
28	Chemicals and allied products	102,329	9,470	111,799	180,459	57	62
29	Petroleum and coal products	197,898	5,157	203,055	224,131	88	91
30	Rubber, miscellaneous plastics products	27,750	2,217	29,967	53,172	52	56
31	Leather, leather products	5,344	199	5,543	10,467	51	53
32	Stone, clay, glass products	23,549	2,580	26,129	48,000	49	54
33	Primary metal industries	94,306	6,338	100,644	141,942	66	71
34	Fabricated metal products	62,600	4,573	67,173	123,661	51	54
35	Machinery, except electric	92,276	8,821	101,097	201,539	46	50
36	Electric, electronic equipment	62,412	6,645	69,057	140,194	45	49
37	Transportation equipment	123,699	10,795	134,494	205,221	60	66
38	Instruments, related products	17,283	2,024	19,307	48,291	36	40
39	Miscellaneous manufacturing	13,172	612	13,784	26,939	49	51

	Cost of Materials (Millions)*	Capital Expenditures, New (Millions)†	Total Material and Capital Expenditures (Millions)	Value of Industry Shipments (Millions)‡	Material Sales Ratio	Total Purchase Sales Ratio
(1971)	356,016	20,940	376,956	670,970	53	56
(1972)	407,418	24,072	431,490	756,534	54	57
(1973)	478,169	26,978	505,147	875,443	55	58
(1974)	581,580	35,696	617,276	1,017,873	57	61
(1975)	597,327	37,262	634,589	1,039,377	57	61
(1976)	681,194	40,545	721,739	1,185,695	57	61
(1977)	782,417	47,459	829,876	1,358,526	58	61
(1978)	877,424	55,209	932,633	1,522,937	58	61
(1979)	999,157	61,533	1,060,690	1,727,214	58	61
(1980)	1,093,567	70,112	1,163,679	1,852,668	59	63
(1981)	1,193,969	78,632	1,272,601	2,017,542	59	63

ALL OPERATING MANUFACTURING ESTABLISHMENTS:

*Refers to direct charges actually paid or payable for items consumed or put into production during the year, including freight charges and other direct charges incurred by the establishment in acquiring these materials. Manufacturers included the cost of materials or fuel consumed regardless of whether these items were purchased by the individual establishment from other companies, transferred to it from other establishments of the same company, or withdrawn from inventory. It excludes the cost of services used, such as advertising, insurance, telephone, etc., and research, developmental, and consulting services of other establishments. It also excludes materials, machinery, and equipment used in plant expansion or capitalized repairs that are chargeable to fixed assets accounts.

†Includes funds spent for permanent additions and major alterations to manufacturing establishments and new machinery and equipment used for replacement purposes and additions to plant capacity if they are chargeable to a fixed-asset account.

‡The received or receivable net selling values, f.o.b. plant, after discounts and allowances, and excluding freight charges and excise taxes. However, where the products of an industry are customarily delivered by the manufacturing establishment (e.g., bakery products), the value of shipments is based on the delivered price.

Source: U.S. Bureau of the Census, 1981 Annual Survey of Manufactures (Washington, D.C.: U.S. Government Printing Office, April 1983), Statistics for Industry Groups and Industries, p. 5, 8, and appendix.

The total purchase/sales ratio went from 56 to 63 percent in this same time period. Any function of the firm that accounts for the use of over half the firm's receipts certainly deserves a great deal of managerial attention.

Profit-Leverage Effect

If, through better purchasing, a firm saves $100,000 in the prices paid to vendors for needed materials, supplies, and services, that $100,000 savings goes directly to the bottom-line (before-tax) account on its profit-and-loss statement. If that same firm sells an additional $100,000 of product, the contribution to profit, assuming a 5 percent before-tax profit margin, would be only $5,000. Clearly, purchase dollars are high powered.

Perhaps an example, using a hypothetical manufacturer, will illustrate this:

- Gross sales $1,000,000
- Purchases (assuming purchases account for 50% of the sales dollar) 500,000
- Profit (assuming a before-tax profit margin of 5%) 50,000

Now, assume this firm was able to reduce its overall purchase cost by 10 percent through better management of the function. This would be a $50,000 additional contribution to before-tax profits. To increase before-tax profits by $50,000 solely through increased sales would require an additional $1,000,000, or a doubling, of sales.

This is not to suggest that it would be easy to reduce overall purchase costs by 10 percent. In a firm that has given major attention to the purchasing function over the years, it would be difficult, and perhaps impossible, to do. But in a firm that has neglected purchasing, it would be a realistic objective. Because of the profit-leverage effect of purchasing, large savings are possible compared to the effort necessary to increase sales by the much larger percentage necessary to generate the same effect on the profit-and-loss statement. Since, in many firms, the sales function already has received much more attention, purchasing may be the last untapped "profit producer."

Return-on-Assets Effect

Firms are increasingly more interested in return-on-assets (ROA) as a measure of performance. Figure 5-1 shows the standard ROA model, using the same figures as in the previous example and assuming, realistically, that inventory accounts for 30 percent of total assets. If purchase costs were reduced by 10 percent, the inventory asset base also would be reduced by 10 percent. The numbers in the boxes show the initial figures used in arriving at the 10 percent ROA performance. The numbers below each box are the figures resulting from a 10 percent overall purchase price reduction, and the end product is a new ROA of 20.6 percent. This is a highly feasible objective for many firms.

Effect on Efficiency

The effectiveness of the purchasing function shows up in other operating results. If purchasing selects a vendor who fails to deliver raw materials or parts that measure up to the agreed-upon quality standards, a higher scrap rate or costly rework, requiring excessive direct labor expenditures, may result. If the vendor selected does not meet the agreed-upon delivery schedule, this may require a costly rescheduling of production, decreasing overall production efficiency or, in the worst case, shutting down the production line while fixed costs continue, even though there is no output.

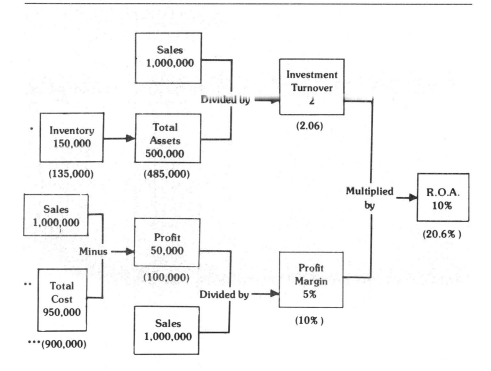

*Inventory is approximately 30 percent of total assets.
**Purchases account for half of total sales, or $500,000.
***(Figures in parentheses assume a 10 percent reduction in purchase costs.)

Figure 5-1. Return-on-Assets Factors

Effect on Competitive Position

A firm cannot be competitive unless it can deliver end products or services to its customers when they are wanted and at a price the customer considers fair. If purchasing doesn't do its job, the firm will not have the required materials when needed and at a price that keeps end-product costs under control.

Some years ago, a major automobile producer decided to buy all its auto glass from one firm (a single source). Some months into the supply agreement, it appeared that the forthcoming labor-contract negotiations might result in a deadlock and a long strike. To protect itself, the auto company built up a 90-day glass stockpile, even though the inventory carrying costs were high, and it had problems finding the physical storage facilities for that much glass. As anticipated, there was a strike in the glass industry, but the union struck only the glass firm supplying that auto producer. The strike lasted 118 days, and the auto producer had to shut down its production lines for over a month.

The auto company had a large net financial loss that year, since that sales loss dropped it below its break-even point. The president explained to the stockholders that the glass strike cost the company the sale of about 100,000 cars (a month's sales). Auto customers evidently were not willing to wait until the strike ended, and they went "across the street" to buy a car made by a competitor. The dealer can tell a customer, "Here's the car. Bring it back in a month, and we'll put the hubcaps on for you," and he'll make the sale. But it's difficult to convince the customer to take the car now and bring it back later for the windshield! Actually, the producer probably lost closer to 500,000 auto sales: if a customer bought another maker's car when he couldn't get the car he wanted and if he liked the different make, he probably returned to the new dealer to buy another car two or three years later, and then did so repeatedly.

Effect on Image

The actions of the purchasing department directly influence the public-relations image of a company. This is particularly true of a company making industrial products, because purchasing has many more outside contacts (with vendors and potential vendors) than the marketing department (which calls on only a limited number of customers). If actual and potential vendors are not treated in a businesslike manner, they will form a poor opinion of the entire company and will communicate this to other firms. This poor image will adversely affect the purchasing firm's ability to get new business and to find new and better vendors.

Training Ground

The purchasing professional, in performing his or her daily activities, interacts with all other areas of the organization. This provides a critical exposure to the needs and operation of the organization. The individual's ability and willingness to take risks and assume responsibility are scrutinized and evaluated when he or she makes decisions under pressure, in an environment of uncertainty and with potentially serious consequences. Many organizations include an assignment in the purchasing area as part of the formal job rotation plan for "fast-track" employees.

Information Source

The daily contacts of the buyer or purchasing manager provide a good deal of potentially useful information about the outside environment. What new products are being developed by competitors? What are the competitors' marketing strategies? New material availability? Is innovative technology being developed? What is the manufacturing strategy of competitors? Who are potential merger and acquisition candidates? What is the direction of the economy? Buyers are in a prime position to answer such questions and feed this intelligence to top corporate management, where it can be evaluated and used in developing and refining the organization's own objectives and strategies.

Organization of Purchasing/Materials Management

A proper organizational structure is necessary for effective performance. This enables the specialization, planning, coordination, communication, and control to make effective materials-acquisition decisions.

Centralization Versus Decentralization

If a firm purchases on a *decentralized* basis, each department manager will handle his or her own purchasing. The advantage to this approach is that the user knows what is needed better than anyone else. Also, it may be faster: when a department needs something, the manager simply picks up the phone and orders it.

But the advantages of *centralized purchasing* outweigh those of decentralized purchasing, and almost all but the smallest of firms are centralized. In centralized purchasing, a separate individual or department is given authority to make all purchases, except, perhaps, the very unusual buy, such as a new company aircraft. Centralized purchasing offers the following advantages.

1. It is easier to standardize the items bought if purchasing decisions go through one central control point.

2. It reduces administrative duplication. Instead of each department head writing a separate purchase order for light bulbs, the purchasing department writes only one order for the firm's total requirement.

3. By combining requirements from several departments, purchasing has the "clout" to go to a vendor and discuss an order quantity that is large enough to really interest the vendor. Often the purchasing department can persuade the vendor to give concessions, such as faster delivery or a quantity discount. There also may be freight savings, because shipment now can be made in carload quantities.

4. In periods of materials shortage, one department does not compete with another department for the available supply and thus drive up the price.

5. It is administratively more efficient for the vendor, who does not need to call on several people within the company. Instead, the vendor "makes a pitch" to the purchasing manager.

6. It provides better control over purchase commitments. Since a large percent of a firm's cash outflow goes for material purchases, a central control point is needed to monitor the aggregate commitment amount at any specific time. Also, purchasing decisions about placement of orders with vendors are sensitive: kickbacks and bribery are possible if orders are issued to unscrupulous vendors. It is easier to prevent such illegal/unethical practices if all decisions on the flow of purchase commitments go through one central "funnel"; this means the spotlight can be focused on the purchasing department, because purchase decisions are not scattered throughout the various departments of the firm.

7. It enables the development of specialization and expertise in purchase decisions and uses time more efficiently. When a department head also tries to be a purchasing agent, the time spent on purchasing probably could be better used in managing the department. Additionally, the department manager will not spend enough time in purchasing to develop any real expertise. A full-time buyer, who can devote undivided attention to purchasing, rapidly develops expert knowledge of purchasing techniques, sources of supply, available and new materials and manufacturing processes, markets, and prices. This development of expertise is the primary reason why almost all firms have centralized the purchasing function.

A variation of centralized purchasing often exists in the multi-plant organization. Here, the firm operates several different producing divisions, which often make different products requiring a different mix of purchased items.

The firm often uses a profit-center management-motivation-and-control technique, in which the division manager is totally responsible for running the division, acts as president of an independent firm, and is judged by profits made by this division. Since material purchases are the largest single controllable cost of running a division and have a direct effect on the efficiency and competitive position of the division, the profit-center division manager insists on having direct authority over purchasing. It would be difficult to hold the division manager responsible for results if the manager lacked decision-making power over the major expenditure area.

This realization has led some firms to adopt decentralized-centralized purchasing, in which the purchasing function is centralized on a division or plant basis but decentralized on a corporate basis. Often a corporate purchasing organization operates in a staff capacity and assists the division purchasing departments in those tasks that are handled more effectively on a corporate basis: (1) establishment of policies, procedures, and controls; (2) recruiting and training of personnel; (3) coordinating the purchase of common-use items, where more clout is needed; and (4) auditing purchasing performance. Figure 5-2 presents a simplified organizational chart for a firm organized on a profit-center basis.

In the 1980s, there has been a gradual movement toward greater centralization of purchasing in the multi-plant organization in order to gain the volume-buying advantages that lead to greater assurance of supply and closer control of purchase prices. *The Purchasing Function: From Strategy to Image,* a study published in 1982 by the Machinery and Allied Products Institute, found that 50 percent of the firms considered had further centralized their purchasing during the past decade; 65 percent predicted even more centralization in the next ten years.

Materials Management

Some organizations have adopted the materials-management organizational concept, where a single manager is responsible for planning, organizing, motivating, and controlling all those activities principally concerned with the flow of materials into an organization. Materials management views material flow as a system. Another way to look at materials management is to consider its major activities:

1.   Anticipating material requirements
2.   Sourcing and obtaining materials
3.   Introducing materials into the organization
4.   Monitoring the status of materials as a current asset

Figure 5-3 shows the specific functions that might be included in a materials-management organization and their relations to other major func-

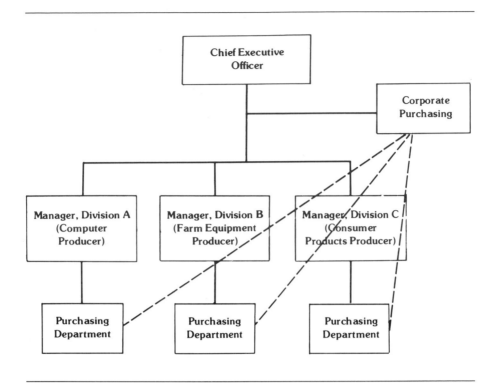

**Figure 5-2. Multi-Division Organization
Structure for Purchasing**

tional areas of the firm. Not all 11 functions shown would have to report to the materials manager; production scheduling, in-plant materials movement, and incoming quality control often are excluded.

The materials-management concept grew out of problems in the airframe industry during World War II. Production of an aircraft requires a large number of individual items, many of which are quite sophisticated and must meet stringent quality standards; these are procured from thousands of vendors located over a wide geographic area. Each item is vital to the total functioning of the end product. The objectives of materials management are: solving materials problems from a total company viewpoint (optimize) by coordinating performance of the various materials functions; providing a communications network; and controlling materials flow. As the computer was introduced into organizations, it provided a further reason to adopt materials management: the materials functions have many common data needs and can share a common data base.

The single-manager materials concept overcomes the shortcomings of the conventional organization, where the various materials functions are or-

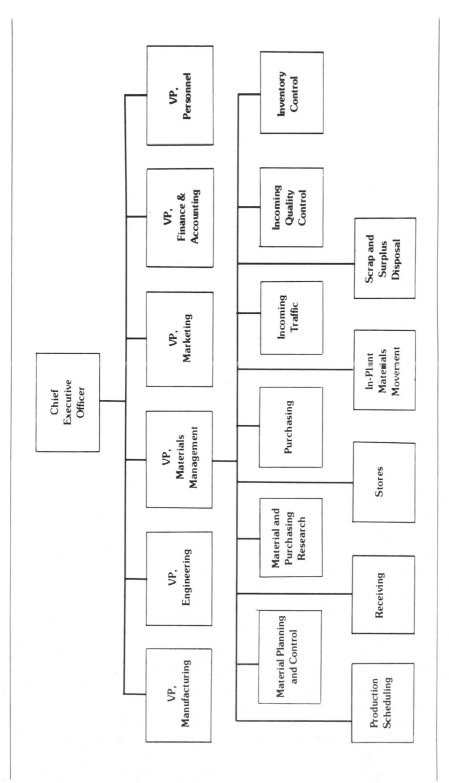

Figure 5-3.   Organization Structure for Materials Management

ganizationally splintered. It recognizes: (1) that materials decisions are additive and not independent of actions elsewhere, (2) the self-interest and potentially conflicting objectives of the individual materials functions, and (3) the need to concentrate authority and responsibility for materials decisions to avoid "buck passing." Materials management, in a formal organizational sense, is not needed in the small organization where the chief executive (normally the owner) makes all the materials decisions and provides the needed coordination and control.

Purchasing Prerogatives

If the purchasing department is to meet the objectives of good purchasing, it must have four key prerogatives.

1. Right to select the vendor. Purchasing should be the expert in knowing who is capable of producing needed items and in analyzing vendor reliability. If someone else selects the vendor, purchasing then is in a sole-source situation and can do little to bargain for an advantageous purchase agreement.

2. Right to use whichever pricing method is appropriate and to determine the price and terms of the agreement. This is one of the main expertise areas of purchasing, which must have room to maneuver if it is to achieve the lowest possible price.

3. Right to question the specifications. Purchasing, which often can suggest substitute or alternate items that will do the same job, is responsible for bringing these items to the attention of the requisitioner. The user makes the final decision on accepting a substitute.

4. Right to control all contacts with potential vendors. Communication with potential vendors must flow through purchasing. If users contact vendors directly, this encourages "back-door selling," in which a potential vendor influences the specifications and creates a sole-source situation. Or, the requisitioner will make commitments to vendors that prevent purchasing from reaching agreements that will give the buying firm the lowest ultimate price. If vendor technical personnel need to talk directly with personnel in the buyer's firm, purchasing will arrange for such discussions and monitor their outcome.

The preceding purchasing prerogatives should be established as matters of company policy and approved by the chief executive officer.

The Standard Purchasing System

The standard purchasing procedure consists of nine steps: (1) recognition of need, (2) description of need, (3) source selection, (4) price determination, (5) purchase-order preparation, (6) follow-up and expediting, (7) receipt and inspection of goods, (8) invoice clearance and payment, and (9) maintenance of records. Performance of these steps varies in detail from company to company, depending on such factors as the status of purchasing within the total organization, competence of purchasing personnel, and the extent to which electronic data processing is used.

Good management dictates that the procedures and policies of purchasing be written out: to assure that the firm follows an approach consistent with its particular needs, to assure consistency and fairness in its purchasing actions, to provide guidance to both buyers and requisitioners in how purchasing is to be handled, and to establish the authority of the purchasing department. A well-managed firm will have an established policy and procedure manual, which is the guidebook for those involved with purchasing. Policies should be established in areas such as: authority to requisition, authority to purchase, use of competitive bids, maintenance of records, acceptance of gifts, use of local suppliers, disclosure of information to vendors, purchasing for employees, charges for tooling, adherence to federal and state laws and regulations, and actions to be taken in the event of discrepancies between the purchase agreement and actual vendor performance.

The key managerial tool used to determine the allocation of time and attention of buying personnel and to establish purchasing strategy is ABC analysis. If a firm arranges any given year's purchase history by listing the one item on which the largest total dollar expenditures were made and then listing in descending dollar value all other items down to the item on which the smallest total dollar expenditures were made, it generally would look like this:

- A items—those 5 percent of the purchased items accounting for 75 percent of the total dollars spent

- B items—those 10 percent of the purchased items accounting for 15 percent of the total dollars spent

- C items—those 85 percent of the purchased items accounting for 10 percent of the total dollars spent

The A items primarily will consist of raw materials and production parts. The B items also will be raw materials and production parts, but the usage amounts and values will be less than for A items. The C items primarily will be maintenance, repair, and operating (MRO) supplies. A given firm may have only 15 items in the A category, 30 items in the B category, and 255 items in the C category, out of a total of 300 items. Since the average annual dollars spent on each A item is 10 times greater than for each B item and about 128 times greater than for each C item, the A item has the largest profit leverage, and this is where most of the time and effort of the purchasing department should be concentrated. A 1 percent saving in the purchase of an A item will produce greater profits than a 99 percent saving on one of the C items. Obviously a 1 percent saving will be more easily attained than a 99 percent saving, which is almost an impossibility. One approach that might be productive is to aggregate several of the individual C items into a family of items (such as all hand tools), thereby moving the family of items into the B category where purchasing can afford to spend more time and effort.

This same ABC analysis technique also applies to other areas of purchasing. Purchase orders segregated by dollar value approximate the ABC breakdown, since most purchasing paperwork is for small-dollar orders. To reduce the quantity and cost of paperwork, a firm should develop a simpler system for processing the small-value, C orders, which require less control since the dollar risk is so much lower. If dollars spent with various vendors are arranged from highest amount by vendor to lowest amount, it also normally will approximate the ABC breakdown. The vendors with whom purchasing does the most business are those on whom the most attention should be spent, because purchasing has the most clout with them and should cultivate good relations with them.

All the routine data collection, processing, and recording functions involved in the nine steps of the standard purchasing procedure can be handled through a computer system. During the past 20 years, the computer has made substantial inroads into purchasing, resulting in three major benefits: (1) reduction of clerical, manual effort; (2) closer control over purchase actions, due to more accurate and more timely decision-making data; and (3) better decisions, resulting from the better data base. Significant changes, beginning in the early 1980s, can be attributed to desk-top, personal-computer systems. The low cost and ready availability of these small, stand-alone systems are making computerization an integral part of the purchasing function in both small and large organizations.

Recognition of Need

The purchasing process is triggered when someone within the organization recognizes that some material, supply, or service is needed and best can be obtained from sources outside the organization. Normally, a need is recognized by a user, such as production, which calculates its requirement for a particular production part based upon its next month's production schedule; or by marketing, which anticipates a need for a new advertising brochure; or by the personnel department, which requires an additional typewriter. This step normally is not performed by purchasing, except in the case of standard, inventory items where purchasing may be responsible for inventory management and resupplying when the stock on hand reaches a preset order point.

In the case of production parts, many firms now use a computerized materials-requirements-planning (MRP) system (discussed in chapter 4) to notify the purchasing department of parts needed, quantities, and need dates.

Description of Need

If purchasing is to fill a recognized need, the user must notify purchasing of the specific characteristics of that need. A simple, two-part form called the purchase requisition generally is used; the original is sent to purchasing, and the requisitioner retains the carbon copy. The information on the requisition should include: date prepared; department preparing and a signature of an individual who can authorize purchase action; description of the item needed; quantity needed; place where delivery is needed; and the date needed. A specific date (month and day) should be indicated; "rush" or "as soon as possible" is not precise enough to guide purchasing. "Rush" may be interpreted by purchasing as a real emergency, and they may pay a higher price to obtain next-day delivery, even though the item really isn't needed for two weeks and could be purchased by normal means and at a much lower price.

The requisitioner need not indicate "suggested price" or "suggested vendor," as purchasing has the expertise to determine the right price and appropriate vendor. If purchasing needs help locating a vendor, it can ask the requisitioner. Also, if the requisitioner feels he must indicate a suggested vendor and price, he probably will contact the vendor directly, opening up the possibility for back-door selling. If, after submitting the requisition, the requisitioner hears nothing from purchasing, he can assume the needed item will arrive by the date specified. If purchasing runs into lead-time problems, they will be discussed with the requisitioner.

If the item is a one-time, immediate-use purchase, the quantity decision is straightforward: purchasing buys the entire quantity for delivery by the needed date. If the item is an MRO item that normally is maintained in inventory or is an item needed over an extended time period, either inventory control or purchasing will make an economic order quantity calculation, as discussed in chapter 6.

If the item is an A category raw material, purchasing may wish to "buy to the market," based upon purchasing's long-term forecast of the supply-and-demand factors. If the item is forecast to be in a market oversupply situation, purchasing may decide to buy only enough to meet immediate needs (called "hand-to-mouth buying") and wait for the price to fall before making additional purchases. If the item is forecast to be in increasingly short supply, purchasing may decide to buy a several-month supply now, in anticipation of a price increase, and put most of it in inventory for later use. Called "forward buying," this decision to buy more than the immediate need is based on data and a realistic estimate of the situation; it is not speculation, which is gambling on price changes when the firm does not have a foreseeable need for the item and is attempting to make a profit from the buying and selling of materials.

Two variations on the standard purchase requisition are the travelling requisition and the bill of materials. The travelling requisition is a cardboard form used when a particular item must be purchased frequently for a given department. The traveller contains a complete description of the item and is sent to purchasing when a resupply of the item is needed by the user, indicating quantity and date needed. Purchasing writes the purchase order; enters data on vendor, price, and order number on the traveller; and sends it back to the requisitioner, who files the card until a subsequent resupply is needed. As many as 24 to 36 purchases can be triggered by this traveller card. Use of the traveller eliminates the recopying of routine description data and substitutes for 24 to 36 individual purchase requisitions, saving paperwork and clerical time. It also provides a complete, cumulative purchase history and use record on one form.

A second variation, the bill of materials (B/M) discussed in chapter 2, is used by firms that make standard, manufactured items over relatively long periods of time; it is a quick way of notifying purchasing of production needs. A B/M for a toaster made by an appliance manufacturer would list the total number or quantity, including an appropriate scrap allowance, of parts or material to make one end unit. Production scheduling then merely notifies purchasing that it has scheduled 18,000 of that model into production next month. Purchasing then will "explode" the B/M (normally by a computerized system) by multiplying through by 18,000 to determine the total quantity of material needed to meet next month's production schedule. Comparison of these numbers with quantities in inventory will give purchasing the "open to buy" figures. The B/M system simplifies the requisitioning process when a large number of frequently needed line items is involved.

The description of the item to be bought is important, because purchasing must understand the requirements if it is to select the most appropriate vendor and clearly communicate quality needs to that vendor. Purchasing's objective is to buy the least expensive item with the attributes needed for the job or application in question. Incoming quality control then will determine whether the item actually received from the vendor meets the specification on the purchase order.

There are several ways quality may be described to purchasing and then by purchasing to the vendor. Each has its peculiar advantages and disadvantages.

Brand or Trade Name

Specifying "Brand X" is a quick means of describing quality, and it is easy to determine whether the right item was delivered. It also gives some assurance that the quality will be consistent over time. Therefore, this is useful in specifying the C category of item, where simple purchase decisions are sought. However, a prime reason manufacturers brand their products is to build up customer loyalty; this permits manufacturers to charge higher prices than those charged for similar, and equally good, unbranded products. The marketing of aspirin is a good example of the price advantage available to a vendor who establishes a brand name in the mind of the buyer.

Market Grade

Many raw materials, such as agricultural and mineral products, have an established grading system that can be used to specify quality. Lumber is a good example. Market grade is a quick and easy method of description, providing the established grading system classifies quality in sufficiently specific intervals to meet a firm's production needs.

Word Picture

This is a complete, written word picture of the characteristics the needed item must possess. Although these can be very exact, they are difficult to compose so that the vendor understands exactly what is requested.

Blueprint

This is a dimensional specification normally used in the purchase of production parts. It is the most exact type of description, but the buyer is responsible for any errors on the print. Blueprints are costly to prepare.

Sample

Why not give vendors samples and ask for duplicates? This is often done when purchasing repair parts, where age or use makes it difficult to locate the original manufacturer. Samples also frequently are used to describe printed matter, such as forms. Sometimes, however, the printer and the buyer disagree about whether the newly delivered printing complies with the sample, particularly if color is involved.

Performance Specification

When purchasing equipment from a vendor who is familiar with the purchaser's needs, it may be enough to tell the vendor what job the needed equipment must perform. For example, a commercial baker might specify a piece of bread-wrapping equipment by indicating the variations in loaf size it must be able to handle, the number of loaves to be wrapped per hour, and the various types of wrap (cellophane, plastic, waxed paper, or plain paper) the machine must use.

Source Selection

One key to good purchasing is the selection of responsible, cooperative vendors. This is perhaps the most important step in the purchasing system, for all else depends on it. The care taken in selecting vendors will depend on the item involved and the dollar risk. Greater care will be taken in the purchase of a new item if it is hard to locate and crucial to the performance of the end product or if it is an A item in which the dollar risk from quality problems or delivery interruptions is high. In purchasing a routine, C-category item, purchasing cannot afford to spend much time, since the risk is small and the savings potential is low.

In some instances, a firm is faced with a make-or-buy decision. For example, instead of buying printed forms, we may decide to purchase the needed equipment and make (print) our requirements in-house. Or, our existing print shop may have excess capacity, and we may decide to fill that capacity with our own needs. Another example would be the reusable hypodermic syringe and needles that are sterilized after use and returned to inventory in a hospital: perhaps it would be more cost-effective to buy disposables. Machined-parts requirements frequently can be made in-house on existing equipment, or they may be purchased from an outside vendor. The make-or-buy decision is based upon a combination of cost, quality, and delivery-service considerations. Purchasing also should provide much of the information for, and should participate in, the make-or-buy decision.

The purchase of a new A item will be handled in four steps, and the process may take several months, compared with selecting a vendor for a C item, on which purchasing may spend only five minutes.

Directory Stage

This is an attempt to make as long a list as possible of vendors considered capable of producing the needed item. The buyer wants several possible vendors on the list, since many will be eliminated later in the evaluation process. The buyer's past experience will be the starting point and probably will produce several vendor names. The buyer then may check with some purchasing counterparts in other purchasing departments, both inside and outside the company. Often, salespeople can provide good leads on available sources. Also, vendor directories list suppliers according to type of product; among these are the telephone book Yellow Pages, *Sweets Catalogs, McRae's Bluebook,* and the catalogs available for specific industries, such as suppliers to the chemical industry. Probably the most used vendor directory is the *Thomas Register of American Manufacturers,* which claims to list all American manufacturers by type of product. The 1985 *Thomas Register* is in 19 oversize volumes that contain about 31,000 pages and list more than 123,000 U. S. manufacturers, 50,000 products and services, and 102,000 brand names and trademarks. These directories, however, do not evaluate the quality or reliability of vendors. Also, buyers, by reading purchasing trade journals and journals in their own industry and by attending various trade shows, will gather general information about possible vendors.

In many firms, the purchasing department makes a concerted effort to find and develop minority vendors—that is, vendors in which at least half the ownership is by minority citizens such as Blacks, American Indians, Orientals, Eskimos, Aleuts, Puerto Ricans, or Chicanos. Some vendor directories, such as *Try Us 1985*, list only minority vendors. Similar emphasis often is given to the use of small vendors (referred to in Public Law 95-507 as "disadvantaged"). This conscious action by purchasing decision makers is a result of a combination of government pressures plus a realization that minority-owned firms and small businesses will only be part of the mainstream of American economic life if purchasing managers select them as suppliers to medium- and large-size buying firms.

Evaluation

Here the buyer gathers information to predict how well the vendor would perform if selected. Again, the amount of effort expended depends upon the importance of the item to be purchased. Obviously, the information the buyer gathers will be imperfect, and some of the vendors finally selected will not perform as predicted. The areas subject to evaluation are almost endless and will depend on the item to be bought. Some key areas to be evaluated are:

1. Reliability. Will the vendor do what it says it will do?

2. Quantity. Can the vendor supply enough to meet our needs?

3. Time element. Can the vendor meet our delivery schedule?

4. Service. Will the vendor provide needed before-and-after-sale support?

5. Quality and quality-control methods. Will the vendor's quality be consistent and meet our requirements? Does the vendor use adequate quality-control methods?

6. Research and development. Is the vendor doing anything to improve its products and production process?

7. Capacity. If our requirements increase, can the vendor handle them?

8. Financial capacity. Is the vendor's financial situation adequate to assure it will be in business long enough to meet our requirements completely? Or will its internal financial situation force it to try to "cut corners"?

9. Labor relations. What has been the vendor's record of work stoppages? What is its future labor situation likely to be?

10. Managerial ability. Is the vendor's management competent and progressive?

11. Warranties. What types of guarantees are provided?

12. Transportation facilities. Does the vendor's transport situation match our needs?

The buyer has several possible means of gathering information to evaluate potential vendors and probably will use a combination of the following data sources to crosscheck conclusions.

1. Past experience. If the buyer has done business with a particular vendor, the outcome of those agreements is a good indication of the future, unless there have been major changes in the vendor's management or operating situation. Certainly, if past dealings were unsatisfactory, the buyer will approach future dealings with that vendor very cautiously.

2. Experience of others. Through contacts with purchasing personnel in other firms, the buyer probably can find out how the vendor has performed on purchase agreements. Purchasing people normally are quite willing to exchange vendor-performance information, if there is no discussion of prices.

3. Obtain a sample. This helps verify a vendor's quality capability. Unless the sample was obtained on a totally random basis, however, its utility is questionable. If the vendor-furnished sample is satisfactory, it merely indicates the vendor is capable of producing a satisfactory item; it doesn't assure that subsequent production quality will be as good as the sample, for the sample probably represents the vendor's best effort. But if the sample is unsatisfactory, that vendor can be eliminated.

4. Salespeople's statements. The buyer will talk with sales representatives and managerial personnel in the vendor firm, asking pertinent questions about the vendor's ability. This free information source should be used, but the buyer knows the vendor has a tendency to say whatever is likely to obtain a purchase order.

5. Plant visit. The best source of information about a new supplier is a visit to the vendor's plant for a firsthand look at the facilities and operating situation and a discussion with vendor personnel. The visit should be planned, and the buyer should know specifically what questions to ask and what data to obtain. After the visit, the buyer should make a complete record of information obtained for later evaluation and comparison. As part of the visit, the buyer should follow the product, starting with the vendor's purchasing department; if the vendor has a poor purchasing system, this will show up later in product quality, delivery,

and/or cost. In many firms, the purchasing department periodically visits every A category vendor to note changes and to maintain close vendor contacts.

6.   Public data. The business press, such as the *Wall Street Journal* and *Business Week,* often contains much useful data on medium-to-large vendors. The buyer may wish to consult the *Wall Street Journal Index* and the *Business Periodical Index* to locate such information. To evaluate a vendor's financial status, the buyer will get a Dun and Bradstreet Credit Report (subject to some error but containing useful information), a corporate annual report, and the Form 10-K and 10-Q reports filed with the Securities and Exchange Commission. In the case of a privately held firm, the buyer may insist on being furnished an audited financial statement.

Approved List

Based on the evaluation, many of the possible vendors probably will be eliminated for one or a combination of reasons. To encourage competition, the buyer should develop an approved list containing at least two firms; three or four would be even better. Being on the approved list does not mean that a vendor will receive an order; that depends on the prices and terms obtained.

Experience Rating

While technically this is not part of the source-selection process, good management dictates that current vendors should be evaluated as a basis for placing future business, dropping vendors, helping vendors improve, and improving the selection process. In many firms, this vendor-performance rating is based on intuition: the buyer simply rates each vendor's performance in categories of "excellent," "good," "needs improvement," or "unsatisfactory." But the intuitive method has two major weaknesses. First, the rating will be unduly influenced by the most recent happenings. If, for example, the vendor was late on this month's shipment, it probably will receive an unsatisfactory rating, even though performance was excellent in all other regards and this was the first time there were any delivery problems. Second, this method does not provide top management with any hard, factual evidence to support a decision to drop a vendor or place more business with that vendor.

As an alternative, some more sophisticated firms have developed a vendor point-rating system that systematically rates vendors on several factors, such as quality, price, and service, based on factual performance records maintained by purchasing and incoming quality control. The ratings are aggregated into a single-number overall rating that can be used to compare total performance among vendors. The individual factor ratings indicate where vendors can improve their performance. To establish such a system, the purchasing department must: (1) identify the important performance factors, (2) determine the relative weight of each factor, (3) assign points based on actual performance records, and (4) total the points. This is a more defensible and useful vendor-performance-evaluation approach. Those firms with a computerized purchasing data system can produce these rating reports easily as an almost free by-product; such a system also can be maintained manually on the A items at a reasonable cost.

Determining Price

While price is only one aspect of the overall purchasing job, it is extremely important. Basically, the purchasing department exists to satisfy the firm's purchase requirements at a lower overall cost than could be accomplished through decentralized purchasing. The purchasing department must be alert to different pricing methods, know when each is appropriate, and skillfully arrive at the price to be paid.

Certain federal and state laws regulate pricing practices. If there is any question of possible violation, the firm's legal counsel should be consulted. The two most important such laws are the Sherman Anti-Trust and Robinson-Patman Acts. The Sherman Anti-Trust Act of 1890 states that any combination, conspiracy, or collusion with the intent of restricting trade in interstate commerce is illegal. This means that it is illegal for vendors to get together to set prices (price fixing) or determine the terms and conditions under which they will sell. It also means that buyers cannot get together to set the prices they will pay.

The Robinson-Patman Act (Federal Anti-Price Discrimination Act of 1936), known as the "one-price law," says that a vendor must sell the same item, in the same quantity, to all customers, at the same price. Some exceptions are permitted, such as a lower price (1) for a larger purchase quantity, providing the seller can cost-justify the lower price through cost accounting data; (2) to move "distress" or obsolete merchandise; or (3) to meet the lower price of local competition in a particular geographic area. The act also states that it shall be illegal for a buyer knowingly to induce or accept a discriminatory price. The courts have been realistic in their interpretation of the law, however, holding that it is the buyer's job to get the best possible price for his company; as long as the buyer does not intentionally mislead the seller into giving a more favorable price than is available to other buyers of the same item, the buyer is not violating the law.

There are basically six methods the buyer can use in establishing price. Each is useful under certain circumstances.

List Price

Most vendors periodically publish a catalog of the items they routinely sell; this normally is accompanied by a price list. The list price is not necessarily the only price the vendor will accept; it is the "asking" price. If the quantity is large enough to make the sale really attractive to the vendor, the buyer normally can obtain concessions, such as a lower selling price, larger trade-in allowance, better cash discount, or free service, such as equipment maintenance. But in the purchase of a C-category item, the buyer does not have the time to pursue a lower price, since a 10 or 20 percent price reduction isn't significant. The buyer probably should pay the list price and use the time saved to do a better job of analyzing and purchasing the A items, where the real profit leverage exists.

Unpriced Purchase Order

Here the buyer sends out the purchase order (PO) complete in all respects, except that no price is shown. What this PO says, basically, is "ship the item as specified and send an invoice at the vendor's normally determined price." Unpriced POs should be used sparingly, for one of the key parameters in any purchase decision should be price, which should be determined prior to placing the order.

In two instances, use of an unpriced PO may be appropriate. In an emergency, such as an equipment breakdown, time may be of greater value than money, and the buyer may wish to get the vendor started immediately, even though price has not been determined. Second, in the purchase of routine, standard items—for example, a gross of #2 lead pencils—from a vendor with whom the company does other business, the buyer may decide merely to say "ship." If the price charged on the invoice is out of line, it will be challenged before payment.

Salesperson's Quotation

A salesperson may quote the buyer a price while in the buyer's office, and the buyer may accept by issuing a PO. Probably there will be no problem, although legally the salesperson presumably doesn't have agency authority, and the offer made by the salesperson legally does not commit the selling company *until* it has been accepted by an officer of that company. If the buyer wishes to accept a salesperson's offer and to know that the offer is legally binding, he or she should ask the salesperson to furnish a letter signed by an officer of the selling company stating that the salesperson possesses the authority of a sales agent.

Market Prices

The reported market prices for many raw material items are listed regularly in many of the trade and business journals, such as *Iron Age* and the *Wall Street Journal*. Such market prices are the reported list prices at which commodities were offered for sale in the past. They are not offers to sell but indications of price levels. They may be used by purchasing as a general gauge of prices, although the astute buyer probably can obtain a better price.

Competitive Bids

This is the most effective means of obtaining a fair price for items bought; the forces of competition are used to assure that the price paid is barely enough to allow the seller to cover costs, plus make a minimum profit. Prospective vendors are sent a request-for-quotation form, which lists all aspects of the needed purchase (specifications, quantity, required date, terms, and conditions). These vendors are asked to respond with the minimum price at which each would be willing to supply this requirement. Each vendor knows that others also are being asked to bid and that the vendor with the lowest quote will get the order. Therefore, the vendor who wants the order should give the buyer an attractive quote. This places considerable pressure on the vendor.

For the bid process to work efficiently, several conditions must be present.

1. There must be at least two, and preferably several, qualified vendors.

2. The vendors must want the business; competitive bidding works best in a buyer's market.

3. The specifications must be clear so that each bidder knows precisely what he is bidding on and so the buyer easily can compare the quotes received from various bidders.

4. There must be honest bidding and no collusion among the bidders.

Negotiation

This most sophisticated and costly means of price determination is used for the purchase of large-dollar items where competitive bidding is not appropriate because one or more of the required conditions is absent. Negotiation requires that the buyer sit down across the table from a vendor; through discussion, they arrive at a common understanding of the essentials of a purchase/sale contract, such as delivery, specifications, warranty, prices, and terms. Because of the interrelation of these factors and many others, it is a difficult art and requires the exercise of judgment and tact. Negotiation is an attempt to reach an agreement that allows both parties to realize their objectives. It is used most often when the buyer is in a sole-source situation; in that case, both parties know that a purchase contract will be issued, and their task is to define a set of terms and conditions acceptable to both. Because of the expense and time involved, true negotiation normally will not be used unless the dollar amount is quite large, probably $50,000 or more.

The buyer normally requests the vendor to present a proposal, accompanied by a cost breakdown, detailing:

1. Direct material costs

2. Direct labor costs

3. Burden or overhead rates and costs

4. Tooling charges

5. Engineering charges

6. General, administrative, and selling costs

7. Profit

The buyer then analyzes these costs (or, if the vendor will not supply a cost breakdown, does a cost buildup, which is quite difficult) and determines areas of disagreement with the vendor's figures. These differences are called "negotiation issues," and the purpose of the negotiation session is to resolve these issues in a manner satisfactory to both parties. Success in negotiation depends upon which party is best able to collect, classify, and analyze pertinent data. Some purchasing organizations have full-time price or cost analysts, whose sole job is to provide good data so the buyer can negotiate from a position of strength (knowledge).

Negotiation often is used to determine the price and terms on both capital-equipment purchases and the purchase of major raw materials over an extended time (long-term contract). In both these situations, the vendor probably will be expending resources over a long future time (perhaps five or ten years) and faces many uncertainties that could cause production costs to accelerate greatly. To protect both the vendor's profit and the buyer's need for assured delivery, the vendor and buyer may need to talk out the various changes in the business environment that might occur and make reasonable provisions for handling each. Often the final, negotiated purchase contract will provide for a price escalation/de-escalation clause as a protection for both parties.

Preparation of the Purchase Agreement

Actual preparation of the purchase order is the least important part of the purchase process; after decisions have been made on specifications, delivery dates, quantity, price, and conditions, PO preparation is largely a clerical process. In some firms, it is done by a computer *after* the pertinent information has been entered into the purchase data base. Because the PO has the status of a legal agreement, it requires a record of an offer (either a PO or a vendor quote) and the corresponding acceptance (a signed vendor acknowledgement copy responding to the PO or a PO accepting the vendor's offer). However, since it is unlikely that legal action to force performance would be taken, except in the case of very large dollar amounts, some firms have eliminated the use of the acknowledgement copy on all but large dollar POs ($5,000 or over) to cut down on paperwork costs.

To reduce administrative costs in PO preparation, many variations can be used. Two examples are blanket orders and blank-check POs. Some firms write a PO with a vendor to cover the entire quantity of a given item for the next year. Terms and conditions are determined at that time. Since it is assured business, the vendor may be willing to give an attractive price and terms. Then, whenever the firm needs additional quantities, it simply sends a delivery "release" to the vendor, quoting the particular blanket-order agreement. The "release" even may be issued by someone other than purchasing, such as inventory control or the user.

With a blank-check PO, the vendor is sent a check along with the PO. When the merchandise is shipped, the vendor enters the amount due on the check and cashes it. This system has certain built-in safeguards: the check can be deposited only to the vendor's account; it must be presented for deposit within 60 days; and the check clearly is marked "Not good for an amount over $1,000." The risk to the buyer is small under these restrictions, and it reduces paperwork on those low-dollar purchases, which typically account for about 90 percent of the paperwork involved in purchasing. Also, it has other major advantages: it saves postage; the buyer can negotiate a larger cash discount in return for instant payment; and it requires complete shipment (no back orders allowed), which reduces the number of receiving reports, inventory entries, and payments. Since the vendor is receiving immediate payment for items shipped, there is a real incentive to ship the order complete.

Follow-up and Expediting

After a PO has been issued to a vendor, the buyer may wish to follow up and/or expedite the order. When the order is issued, an appropriate follow-up date is indicated. In some firms, purchasing has full-time follow-up and expediting personnel.

Follow-up is the routine "tracking" of an order to assure that the vendor will be able to meet delivery promises. If problems in terms of quality or delivery develop, the buyer needs to know this as soon as possible so that appropriate action can be taken. Follow-up requiring frequent inquiries to the vendor on progress and possibly a visit to the vendor's facility will be done only on large-dollar and/or long lead-time buys.

Expediting is the application of pressure to get the vendor either to meet an original delivery promise or to deliver ahead of schedule. It may involve the threat of order cancellation or withdrawal of future business if the vendor cannot meet the agreement. Expediting should be necessary on only a small percentage of the POs issued; if the buyer has done a good job of analyzing vendor capabilities, only reliable vendors who will perform according to the purchase agreement will be selected. And if the firm has done an adequate job of planning its material requirements, it should not need to ask a vendor to move up the delivery date except in unusual situations. Of course, in times of scarcity, the expediting activity assumes greater importance. The use of MRP systems (see chapter 4) allows purchasing to make more timely decisions on where and when expediting is needed and whether vendor deliveries should be stretched out.

Receipt and Inspection

When goods arrive, a check (normally a simple count) must be made to verify that the quantity received is as ordered. In addition, if it is a production raw material or an item for which precise specifications have been supplied to the vendor, verification of the quality of the goods delivered must be made. Chapter 7 discusses the importance of incoming quality levels and the methods for verification. International competition and the use of concepts such as just-in-time (JIT) manufacturing systems have intensified the need to insure that purchased materials meet the requisitioner's quality and quantity specifications. In the medium- to large-size organization, there typically are separate receiving and incoming inspection departments. In the smaller organization, the purchasing department may handle receipt and inspection, although this compromises the checks and balances needed for adequate control.

Invoice Clearance and Payment

The vendor must receive payment for the delivery of satisfactory items. If cash discounts are available—for example, 2 percent cash discount if payment is made within 10 days, net amount due in 30 days—the paperwork flow must be handled expeditiously. A 2 percent/10, net 30 cash discount term amounts to a real annual interest rate of approximately 36 percent.

Payment will be made by accounts payable. Purchasing could handle the invoice clearance, but the clerical nature of this task dictates that it be done in accounts payable, providing it has the pertinent data for the task. Basically, the purchase order, the receiving report (showing quantities delivered), the incoming inspection report (verifying quality), and the vendor invoice are compared. If all documents agree or are not out of agreement by more than a set amount, such as either ten dollars or 5 percent of PO value, the vendor is paid. If the documents don't agree, then the whole transaction goes back to the buyer for resolution.

Some companies with a computerized data system in purchasing use an invoiceless payment system: the PO goes into the computer on release, and the receiving report and incoming inspection data also go into the computer daily. The computer merely cycles through all POs each night; whenever it finds one in which the PO, receiving report, and inspection report all agree, it triggers a check to be written within a set number of days after the material was received. If the documents don't agree, then the whole transaction goes to purchasing. The advantage of this system is that the handling of the invoice is eliminated. This system also makes it more difficult for vendors to escalate prices after they receive the purchase order, for the PO is the action document that determines the price to be paid.

Maintenance of Records

Before the purchase transaction can be filed away and closed, the records of the purchasing department should be updated so they will be timely and accurate for future use. These records can be maintained in either a computerized or a manual data base. Numerous records might be kept for evaluation, review, and control purposes. The following are the four most important.

1. PO Log. Purchase orders are registered and controlled by serial number. A look at the log will identify any particular PO and show its status. When the order is closed, the log is updated to show completion.

2. Vendor file. Records should be kept on performance and evaluation of capability of those relatively few vendors with whom purchasing does the majority of business. These data permit a vendor-performance evaluation for later decisions.

3. Commodity file. A purchase-history file should be maintained, by commodity, on all major purchased commodities. It should indicate purchase date, vendor, quantity, price and terms, and the current order status.

4. Contract file. This shows all national contracts, blanket orders, and/or annual agreements that have been established, and performance under the contracts. For example, if the annual agreement commits the firm to purchase a total quantity over the next 12 months, the firm must know its current status. Also, a central reference point is needed to determine exactly what purchase items are under contract and should not be handled on an individual basis.

Current and Future Developments

Changes in the environment, the competitive marketplace, and technology, coupled with top management's growing awareness of the profit potential of effective purchasing and materials management, are causing several fundamental changes. Additional changes, some predictable and some not currently identifiable, undoubtedly will occur, providing an exciting challenge to the professionals performing in this area. Six of these developments are highlighted here.

Single Sourcing

Many items are available from several reliable sources; when a conscious decision is made to place *all* the requirement with only one vendor, this is called single sourcing. This gives the buyer the advantage of volume leverage, often resulting in a substantially lower ultimate purchase price. The potential problem is the risk of nondelivery caused by problems in the single-source supplier's plant or with the transportation system. For single sourcing to be effective, the buyer must do an extremely thorough job of analyzing the vendor's management and capabilities and of negotiating a complete contractual agreement, in which all contingencies are anticipated. Japanese industry has used this approach for years; indeed, it is a key element in the just-in-time production system (see chapters 4 and 6). U.S. manufacturers are incorporating single sourcing into their new systems for automobile production. For example, on the production of one of the new model cars, one exhaust-system manufacturer has been selected as a single source; truckload shipments of mufflers must arrive at the auto assembly plant at 2¼-hour intervals throughout each work shift.

Public Purchasing

Governmental purchases of goods and services are big business, deserving a major amount of attention by government administrators. The federal government buys about $300 billion worth of goods and services annually (about 65 percent of which is for national defense); state and local government purchases are over $400 billion each year. Thus, an overall reduction of 10 percent in prices paid would result in an annual savings for the taxpayer of some $70 billion. Starting in 1978 in California with the passage of Proposition 13, often referred to as "the taxpayers' revolt," and followed by the 1983 recommendation of the President's Private Sector Survey on Cost Control task force (called the Grace Commission), much attention has been focused on improving the purchasing practices of governmental units. These taxpayer studies and actions underscore two points: government buying does not differ basically from private-sector purchasing, and governmental units should follow the principles and practices of efficient purchasing outlined in this chapter in order to obtain maximum value for each public dollar spent.

Purchasing Transportation Services

The total transportation cost in the United States for movement of goods is estimated at nearly 10 percent of gross national product, or over $330 billion per year. A large share of that amount (perhaps half, or $165 billion) is payment for moving goods from a vendor's facility to the point where the buyer needs them. Depending on the type of good, transportation may account for as much as 40 percent of the total cost of an item, particularly if it is of low value and bulky, such as construction materials. Before the 1980s, decisions about the mode of transport (air, rail, water, pipeline, or truck), routing, and tariff (price) were primarily clerical. In the past five years, however, Congress has deregulated almost all modes of transportation, and the effects of deregulation have made carrier-selection and pricing decisions far more complex and important today.

The 1977 Air Cargo Act deregulated air cargo; the 1978 Airline Deregulation Act began the deregulation of passenger air transportation, permitting the entry of new airlines, routes, and ticket-price competition. The 1980 Motor Carrier Act relaxed the Interstate Commerce Commission regulation of trucking, allowing easier entry of new firms, new routes and schedules, and flexibility in setting rates. The 1980 Staggers Rail Act gave railroads greater freedom to set rates and to enter into long-term contracts with shippers; piggyback service was completely deregulated. The 1982 Bus Regulatory Reform Act removed all regulation of package express after 1985.

As a result of deregulation, many large organizations have separate transportation departments, often reporting to purchasing or to the materials manager. In the medium-size or smaller organization, where the number of traffic decisions does not warrant a full-time traffic specialist, the buyer or purchasing manager makes traffic decisions. In any event, the buying company is paying for transportation services. The transport decision maker must be able to make value analyses of alternatives, conduct cost/price analyses, negotiate with carriers, consolidate freight and obtain volume discounts, evaluate carrier performance, explore the possibility of using different transport modes, and develop compatible working relationships with selected carriers.

Buyer-Supplier Computer Information Exchange

The use of the micro-computer in purchasing allows the purchasing data base to tie directly into a supplier's data base through the telecommunications system, using a computer modem. This helps both buyer and supplier obtain much more timely and accurate information, permitting paperwork reduction and better purchasing decisions. The cost of such direct data communication has decreased rapidly over the past few years, putting this technology within reach of almost all firms. With such communication links with suppliers, the buyer quickly can obtain price quotes, determine availability of items in a supplier's stock, transmit a PO, obtain follow-up information, provide information about changes in purchase requirements caused by schedule revisions, obtain service information, and send letters and memos.

Foreign Purchasing

The amount of purchases U.S. firms make from vendors outside North America has grown markedly in the 1980s. In the middle 1980s, U.S. buyers paid between $200 and $300 billion to foreign vendors each year. The reasons for specific foreign-sourcing decisions are many and varied, including: lower overall costs from foreign sources; the strong U.S. dollar; more consistent quality; unavailability of items, such as chrome ore, domestically; more predictable delivery schedules; advanced technology; and better technical service. In addition, when a sale of U.S.-made product—for example, an aircraft or a computer—is made in a foreign country, the foreign buyer may demand that the U.S. firm spend a specific percentage (often 50 percent) of the selling price with vendors in that country. This is called "countertrade," and it has become a common practice for many firms. As the world grows smaller, commercially, the purchasing department is becoming involved in sourcing and pricing with vendors all over the world. This brings new problems and opportunities that require a sophisticated degree of purchasing analysis and professionalism: the location and evaluation of foreign suppliers; extended lead times; expediting; currency fluctuations; payment methods; tariffs and duties; and legal, linguistic, and cultural differences are all concerns of the purchasing professional engaged in foreign transactions.

Purchasing/Materials Management Strategy

Over the past 80 years, the purchasing function has evolved from a clerical activity to one that uses complex processes to provide information for effective decision making by professional purchasing managers who perform the function in an asset-management context. This change has stimulated the development of strategies to maximize the effectiveness of purchasing/materials management and, thus, overall organizational effectiveness. A strategy looks at the long-term future (often from 5 to 20 years) rather than simply reacting to the current situation and requirements.

The three major categories of purchasing strategies are: (1) assurance of supply, to meet future supply needs effectively and economically; (2) supply support, to maximize the likelihood that the considerable knowledge and capabilities of suppliers are made available to the buying organization; and (3) environmental change, to anticipate and recognize shifts in the total environment (economic, organizational, people, legal, governmental, and systems) so they can be turned to the long-term advantage of the buying organization. Among the more promising strategy opportunities are: developing new supply sources (supplier development), buying an ownership interest in a supplier, foreign sourcing, single sourcing, promoting vertical integration by buying out a supplier, buyer-supplier data sharing, using the futures market (hedging), systems contracting, consignment buying, risk sharing with suppliers on new products/projects, make/buy, and supplier quality assurance/certification programs. To integrate some of these substrategies into a viable, overall purchasing strategy will be a difficult task but one that is imperative for the survival of many of our current organizations into the twenty-first century.

References

Aljian's Purchasing Handbook. 4th ed. New York: McGraw-Hill, 1982.

Coates, Paul H. *Handbook of International Purchasing.* 2nd ed. Boston: Cahners Books, 1976.

Dobler, Donald W.; Lee, Lamar, Jr.; and Burt, David N. *Purchasing and Materials Management.* 4th ed. New York: McGraw-Hill, 1984.

Heinritz, Stuart F., and Farrell, Paul V. *Purchasing: Principles and Applications.* 6th ed. Englewood Cliffs, NJ: Prentice-Hall, 1981.

Leenders, Michiel R.; Fearon, Harold E.; and England, Wilbur B. *Purchasing and Materials Management.* 8th ed. Homewood, IL: Richard D. Irwin, 1985.

Messner, William. A. *Profitable Purchasing Management.* New York: AMACOM, a division of American Management Associations, 1982.

Zenz, Gary J. *Purchasing and the Management of Materials.* 5th ed. New York: John Wiley & Sons, 1981.

Discussion Questions

1. "The purchasing function is not profit making but, rather, profit taking, since its job is to spend company funds." Is this statement correct? Explain.

2. What is the overall price objective of purchasing?

3. "The most important part of the complete purchasing procedure is the writing of the PO, for this determines the agreement between seller and buyer." Do you agree? Explain.

4. What are the various means of price determination? Give an example of an item you would buy using each method.

5. Why have most organizations centralized the purchasing function?

6. Which of the eight objectives of purchasing is most important? Why?

7. Should an organization expend resources on strategic materials planning? Under what conditions?

8. Will the purchasing function become more or less centralized over the next five years?

9. Is foreign purchasing a viable alternative for most U.S. firms? What are the problems, and how can they be handled?

Chapter 6

Inventory Management

Every organization must manage inventories of one form or another. These inventories may be raw material, parts, partly completed products, finished products, or simply office supplies. The management of raw materials is critical to the oil refiner. Partly completed components and purchased parts are important inventories for an assembler of finished products. Rapid turnover of finished goods is a cornerstone to the successful retailer. Having office supplies available when needed is important to the office manager. No one can ignore the challenges of inventory management.

The essence of inventory management can be summarized in three questions:

1. How much of a specific item should we make or buy at one time?

2. When should we make or buy a specific item to replenish our stocks?

3. How should we store our stocks until they are used?

This chapter will consider these questions by discussing the functions of inventories, the costs and tradeoffs involved in the use of inventories, and some of the decision-making tools and concepts used in inventory management.

The Functions of Inventories

Inventories contribute to the economy and efficiency of an organization in many ways, such as allowing economies of scale, improving customer service, and allowing greater flexibility in scheduling production.

Economies of Scale

In many instances, it is more economical to deal in large volumes. For example, if 55 gallons of paint will be needed during the next two months, it usually will cost less to buy one 55-gallon drum of paint than to buy 55 separate 1-gallon cans as they are needed. The savings result from quantity price discounts and reduced administrative costs of purchasing.

A similar situation arises in manufacturing when choosing the method of producing a product. If it is expensive to prepare (set up) equipment for a particular job, a manufacturer may decide to make a whole year's supply at one time instead of preparing the equipment several times during the year. For example, assume the construction of a housing development consists of five homes. To build the homes, it is necessary to pour five concrete slabs. Since it is costly to get the required equipment to the construction site, it would be considerably cheaper to do all the slabs at one time.

The purchasing and construction examples assume that the most economical quantities to buy or to make are 55 gallons of paint and five concrete slabs, respectively. The purchased quantity is referred to as the economic order quantity (EOQ) and the manufactured lot as the economic lot size (ELS). Moreover, both quantities are referred to as cycle stocks, from the cyclic behavior of the inventory levels. When the 55 gallons of paint are received, the inventory goes up by 55 units. As the paint is used, the inventory declines until we have used all the paint. Assuming an ongoing need for paint, a new order for 55 gallons will arrive when the inventory balance reaches zero. Hence, the cycle stock goes from 55 units down to zero units and then back to 55 units over and over again.

Improving Customer Service

Inventories of finished goods allow customers to compress the time between their decision to purchase an item and actually taking delivery. Without inventories, the buyer would have to place an order and then wait while the item was produced. Compare purchasing an automobile off the showroom floor with ordering a car from the factory. Buying from the finished-good inventory on the showroom floor means possession in a matter of hours. The factory order may delay possession for weeks or months, or perhap the sale will be canceled. The potential for lost sales is a major incentive to carry finished-goods inventories. This incentive is particularly strong when the manufacturing process takes a long time relative to the patience of the customer.

Smoothing Production with Seasonal Inventories

Many products have seasonal demand patterns. For example, snow skis are in great demand just prior to and during the winter months; conversely, water skis are in demand during the summer months. Some companies attempt to smooth out their production by manufacturing complementary products, such as snow and water skis, but this is not always a desirable or complete solution. Others will adjust their production to the demand pattern, but such an adjustment usually requires letting an excessive amount of equipment lie idle much of the year, as well as hiring and laying off employees.

To avoid the disruptive effects of seasonal demand, a company may choose an inventory solution. In this case, production is set at the level rate needed to meet the average annual demand. In the off seasons, production is greater than demand, and inventories are built up. During the peak demand months, production remains the same, which is lower than the demand, and the excess demand is supplied from finished-product inventories that were produced in advance.

Decoupling

Decoupling means to separate tasks or operations that normally are linked directly to one another. The earlier example of the automobile purchase illustrates a decoupling of the sales process from the manufacturing process. Decoupling is equally important within the manufacturing process. Visualize a three-step assembly line that prepares a mass mailing of company advertisements. The first operator addresses an envelope and passes it to a second operator. Operator 2 folds the advertisement, stuffs the envelope, and passes it to a third operator. Operator 3 stamps and sorts the envelope by zip code. If Operator 2 is faster than Operator 1, or if Operator 3 is faster than Operator 2, or if anyone has problems, the assembly operation bogs down. By placing work-in-process inventories between each operation, decoupling is achieved. Such inventories permit each operator to vary speed, have problems, or take breaks without disrupting the operations that precede or follow.

Stock-out Protection

When a customer goes to a store, a mechanic goes to a material stockroom, or a clerk goes to an office-supply stockroom, each expects to obtain specific items. To be out of stock risks lost sales, production stoppage, or a slowdown in office procedures. To reduce these risks, companies carry inventories called buffer stocks or safety stocks, which are designed to combat the problems caused by late deliveries of resupply orders and unusually high usage rates by customers, mechanics, or office personnel.

Economics of Inventory Management

The management of inventory focuses on the appropriate achievement of decoupling, buffering, production smoothing, and desired service levels at the least cost. Certain costs are involved in obtaining and carrying inventories.

These costs must be minimized if the firm is to achieve economically the various functions of inventories. These costs, which must be justified by the benefits from decoupling and production smoothing, include ordering costs, setup costs, and carrying costs.

Ordering Costs

Every time a company purchases raw materials, parts, or supplies, costs are incurred. The previous chapter discussed the preparation of a purchase order, follow-up and expediting tasks, invoice clearance and payment procedures, as well as the record-keeping requirements of purchasing. Each of these activities requires employee time, which represents a cost. Even before the purchasing cycle begins, costs are incurred. The stock-keeper and users of purchased items must expend time and effort to determine what materials to requisition. This effort may consist of checking inventory records or stock bins to determine if more material is needed. In other cases, production scheduling effort results in a bill of materials that initiates the purchasing cycle. Each of these activities is a component of the ordering cost.

For a cost element to be considered part of the ordering cost, it must, first of all, be a relevant cost: if the order didn't exist, then the cost would not occur. And, second, the cost is *not* a function of the size of the order.

For example, the time and the corresponding wages required to process an order are relevant costs if that time (wages) could be saved or used elsewhere if the order were not processed. On the other hand, if the person processing orders is paid for eight hours and is busy for only four, adding two hours of ordering processing to the person's job will not increase the company's costs. This assumes that the idle time will not be put to any other use. In this case, the order processing does not incur a cost (at least in the short run). To the extent that additional order processing leads to more personnel and wages, these costs become relevant.

The second characteristic of ordering costs stresses that the cost element remains substantially the same regardless of the size of the order. For example, it will cost about the same amount to process an order for 1 ton of steel as for 2 tons, 10 tons, or 100 tons.

Setup Costs

Every time a manufacturer shifts from producing one product to another, certain changeover costs occur. These include removing leftover material from the previous production run, readjusting or modifying the work stations, assigning new work crews, and testing the new setup to assure that it performs properly. These costs are subject to the same two criteria as ordering costs. They must be relevant costs that (1) vary with the number of setups, but

(2) not with the number of units that will be produced after the setup has been made. For example, it may take a mechanic two hours to obtain, attach, and adjust the appropriate jigs and fixtures on a machine for a particular job. This setup time is required whether 1 unit or 1,000 units are to be produced. Moreover, the mechanic may be working on overtime, so the time spent on the setup is clearly a relevant cost.

Inventory Carrying Costs

There are two categories of carrying costs: (1) those that are proportional to the value of the inventory and (2) those that are proportional to the physical characteristics of the inventory. In either case, the costs of carrying inventory vary with the amount stocked.

Costs that vary with the dollar value in inventory are:

1.   Cost of capital tied up in stocks

2.   Insurance premiums on inventories

3.   Property taxes on inventories

4.   Obsolescence, deterioration, and damage to stocks

5.   Pilferage

Carrying costs that are proportional to the physical characteristics of the commodity are:

1.   Storage space

2.   Storage labor

These costs will increase as the amount stocked increases if space costs actually change with the storage required and if handling actually increases. These relationships are not always clear-cut. For example, if excess warehouse space is available, then moderate increases in inventory will occupy only space that has little or no alternative use. In this case, the storage-space costs do not increase. If the space is rented on the basis of space actually used, however, then a storage-space cost is relevant. Similarly, if larger inventories lead to more rehandling and more time spent performing physical inventories, then the additional labor costs of carrying inventory are relevant.

Managing the Economic Trade-offs

To minimize inventory costs, it is necessary to find the order quantity or production run that spreads the ordering/setup costs over as many units as possible without incurring excessive carrying costs. The larger the order quantity, the lower the ordering cost per unit. The larger order quantity, however, leads to higher average and peak inventories. The higher average inventory results in high costs due to the dollar value in stock. The peak inventories can be particularly significant (and costly) if storage space is limited.

Finding the best balance between ordering and carrying costs requires a great deal of data collection. The data then can be analyzed and appropriate decisions made. Because data collection and analysis can be expensive, the firm should attempt to reduce the size of that task. One approach is to direct attention to those inventory items that are most significant dollarwise and are, therefore, the most important inventory items.

ABC classification of inventory.   Because inventory control requires time and effort, it is important to direct these resources toward those inventory items that represent significant savings opportunities. The ABC principle (see chapter 5) identifies those inventory items that represent the greatest dollar value. Management, armed with this information, then can allocate control effort proportional to the significance of the inventory class (see figure 6-1). For example, detailed inventory records are kept and frequently reviewed for the most important inventory items, class A. Less frequent reviews and larger buffer stocks can be tolerated in the control of class-B inventory items. In the case of the least significant inventory items, class C, a minimal amount of dollars is spent in control activities.

The ABC analysis is quite straightforward. The annual usage of each inventory item is established in dollar terms. This list of items is then ranked on the basis of dollar volume, highest to lowest. The class-A items consist of approximately the top 10 to 20 percent of the item list—for example, the top 200 dollar-volume items of an inventory consisting of 1,000 items. The class-A items generally account for about 80 percent of the annual dollar volume flowing through inventory. Similarly, class-B items consist of the next 30 to 40 percent of the items and account for another 15 percent of the annual dollar value. The remaining 50 percent of the inventory items accounts for a mere 5 percent of the dollar value. Since it costs about the same to control a C item as it does to control an A item, it is clear where our first priority should be.

Economic Order Quantity Model

The economic order quantity (EOQ) model determines the number of units to purchase that will minimize the combined costs of ordering and carrying the inventory. To use the EOQ model, certain assumptions must be met.

1.   The annual usage of the item is known and constant, or at least very close to constant, over the entire period.

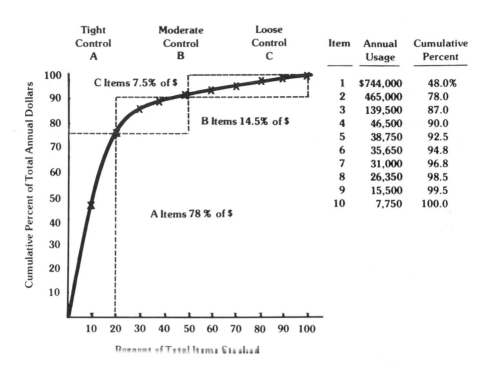

Item	Annual Usage	Cumulative Percent
1	$744,000	48.0%
2	465,000	78.0
3	139,500	87.0
4	46,500	90.0
5	38,750	92.5
6	35,650	94.8
7	31,000	96.8
8	26,350	98.5
9	15,500	99.5
10	7,750	100.0

Figure 6-1.   ABC Classification of Inventories

2.   Material, when received, comes in all at once.

3.   The order-cost factor includes all those relevant costs incurred when an order is placed, and these costs are not influenced by the size of the order.

4.   The carrying-cost factor includes all the relevant costs that vary proportional to the size of the order.

5.   No quantity discounts are considered.

The first two assumptions are reflected in figure 6-2. The representation of line AB as a straight line is consistent with constant usage. The vertical line BC shows that replenishment of stock is received in one lump and enters stock immediately upon receipt. Minor deviations from these assumptions, as illustrated by lines CD and DE, do not seriously affect the model. Line FG shows the effect of delayed resupply. The result would be negative inventory

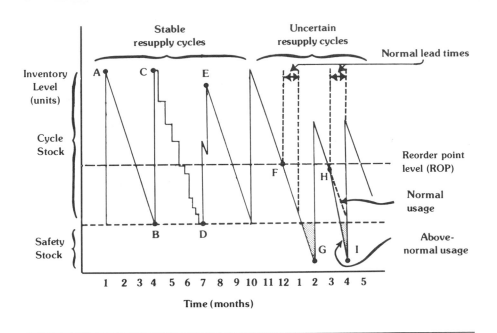

Figure 6-2. Inventory Levels over Time

(a stock-out) if reserves (safety stock) were not available. Line HI illustrates the consequences of above-average usage during the resupply cycle. These issues are discussed in more detail later in this chapter.

The Total Inventory Cost Equation

The basic inventory-cost equation combines the ordering or setup costs for a year (or some other time period) with the carrying costs based on the average inventory level. To be complete, purchase cost also is included.

The number of orders per year is merely the annual demand divided by the number of units in each order. The result is the number of times the ordering costs are incurred. The ordering cost(s) is a constant and does not vary with order quantity (Q), thus incorporating assumption three.

The order quantity (Q) represents the cycle stock. If a zero safety stock is assumed, inventory will cycle from 0 units to Q units and back to 0 units. The assumption of uniform usage results in an average inventory of Q/2 units. This is the average inventory over the entire year, which is multiplied by the carrying cost per unit (IC) to get the annual carrying cost. As Q increases, the carrying cost increases, thus assumption four is incorporated into the equation.

Total Cost = Ordering Costs + Carrying Costs + Purchase Cost

$$TC = \left(\frac{D}{Q}\right)S + IC\left(\frac{Q}{2}\right) + CD$$

TC = total cost
 D = annual demand (units)
 S = ordering or setup cost
 Q = order quantity (units)
 I = carrying cost as a %
     of unit cost
 C = item unit cost (purchase price)

$\frac{D}{Q}$ = number of orders per year

IC = carrying cost per unit per
     year

$\frac{Q}{2}$ = average inventory

EOQ Formula

Simple calculus is used to find the value of Q, which will minimize the total-cost equation. The resulting formula is:

$$EOQ = \sqrt{\frac{2DS}{IC}}$$

The EOQ quantity represents the optimum order size when the assumptions of the model are reasonably well met. One assumption that often is not met is that price is not affected by the order size. Another violation of the assumptions occurs when an order is received over a significant period of time. This situation will be considered later in this chapter in the discussion of economic lot sizes. The price issue is considered next.

EOQ with Discounts

Price discounts affect two components of the total-cost equation, the carrying cost and the purchase cost. Both costs are functions of the price. Price discounts lead to a family of cost curves, one curve for each price. Each curve applies to the range of order sizes for which the associated price is relevant. Figure 6-3 shows a contrast between the total-cost curve without discounts and the family of curves when there are three prices, based on two price-break points.

An iterative process is required to find the optimum order quantity when quantity discounts are available.

1. Compute the EOQ using the best price. If the result is large enough to obtain the best price, then this is the optimum, and the computation stops. If this EOQ falls below the relevant price break, go to the next step.

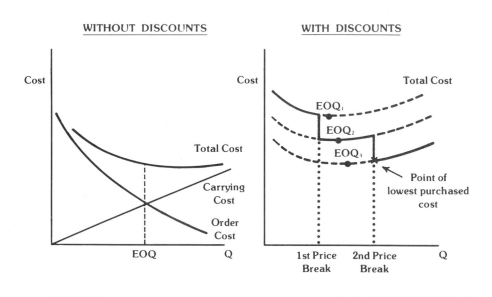

Figure 6-3. Inventory Costs With and Without Quantity Discounts

2. Compute the EOQ using the next best price. Check the result to see if it falls in the relevant range. If EOQ is below the relevant price break, redo this step at the next lower price.

3. Once an EOQ has been found that is consistent with the price obtainable at that order quantity, the final step can be taken. This step is required to determine if an increase to one of the break points offers enough savings to offset the increased carrying costs. Therefore, it is necessary to compute the total cost at the valid EOQ point and at the price breaks above the EOQ point. The decision is made to order the quantity with the lowest total cost. Figure 6-3 shows that EOQ(2) is in the relevant range but that the total cost at the second price break is lower and, therefore, is the optimum order quantity.

Economic Lot-Size (ELS) Formula

In the case of parts manufactured within the firm, the assumption of immediate, one-lump replenishment often is unrealistic. The replenishment actually occurs over the period of the production run, which may be days or weeks. Figure 6-4 shows the basic pattern followed by the level of inventory on hand.

When the entire lot size is not delivered instantaneously, the peak inventory is lower. Specifically, it is lowered by the amount used during the

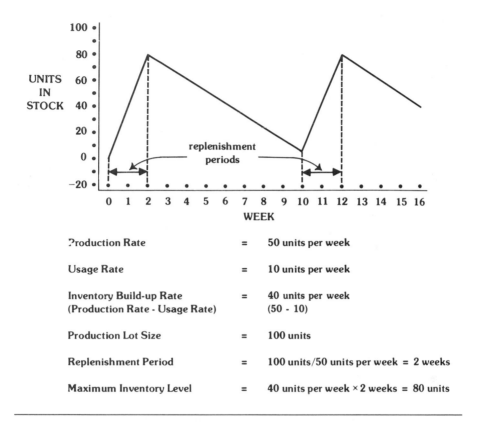

Figure 6-4.   Inventory Levels with Replenishment
Spread over Time

time required to produce the lot. This period is equal to the lot size (100 units) divided by the production rate (50 units per week), or two weeks in this example. In figure 6-4, the usage during the production period is 10 units per week, or 20 units in total. Therefore, instead of 100 units (the lot size), the peak inventory is only 80 units. The average inventory carried is Q/2, or 40 units. Incorporating these changes into the total-cost equations and developing the optimum lot size (as done for EOQ) gives:

$$TC = \frac{DS}{Q} + IC\left(1 - \frac{d}{p}\right)\frac{Q}{2}$$

$$ELS = \sqrt{\frac{2DS}{IC\left(1 - \frac{d}{p}\right)}}$$

Symbols explained:
d = usage rate (units per time period)
p = production rate (units per time period)
D = annual demand
S = setup costs
IC = carrying cost per unit per year
Q = lot size
ELS = economic lot size

With the exception of the replenishment modification, all the assumptions of the EOQ formula still apply.

Periodic Review Model

It is sometimes more convenient to check inventory levels at regular intervals and order those items expected to run out before the next review is scheduled. By checking all inventory items or a class (for example, those items supplied by one vendor) at one time, the firm can combine all orders to a vendor and consolidate freight loads. Moreover, this approach does not require a perpetual inventory system—that is, one that keeps track of the inventory levels at all times. The other side of the coin reveals that more safety stock is required, and, if care is not taken, unbalanced work loads can be placed on inventory and purchasing personnel. Also, the review interval should reflect the economic order quantity. The desired interval for different items will vary, and this is in conflict with the consolidation advantages.

Assuming a review period of a month, the following procedure would apply:

1. Take a physical count of the items to be reviewed.

2. If the inventory balance of an item is less than a specified level, for example, (s) units, then order enough to raise the level to (S) units. Small (s) would be based on the demand over the review interval plus the normal lead time and the desired safety stock. Large (S) is the upper limit needed to cover the period between the current order and the next desired order review. If enough is on hand or on order, then do not place an order.

This approach results in unequal order quantities and requires more safety stock to obtain the same service level than would be needed if the EOQ model is used. However, simpler record keeping and consolidation advantages may make it desirable, particularly for class-C inventory items.

Sensitivity of EOQ and ELS

How accurate must the cost estimates and demand forecasts be? Figure 6-3 shows that the total-cost curve is quite flat in the area of the EOQ. This suggests that moderate departures from the EOQ will not be very costly. This observation is significant, considering how expensive it would be to develop extremely accurate estimates of all relevant costs. The insensitivity of the formulas permits the valid grouping of stock items and estimating the costs for groups as a whole. This approach, along with the ABC classification, can reduce substantially the cost of determining EOQ and ELS.

Safety Stocks and Uncertainty

If all the estimates and assumptions were realized in practice, then efficient inventory management would be relatively easy. But demand rarely is uniform and completely predictable, and stocks are not always replenished on time. The specific function of safety stocks is to reduce the risk of stock-outs due to unexpected demand and/or late resupply. In order to set the level of safety stock, we must consider supply lead times, reorder points, and desired service levels.

Lead Times

Lead time refers to the time between the recognition of a need for and the receipt of the desired material. The purchasing lead time could consist of the requisition review time, the vendor-selection process, order preparation, mail-transit time, supplier-order-processing time, supplier-setup and manufacturing time, shipment time, receiving time, and the time to make the item available from stock. If the time to perform some or all of these elements varies, then some additional stock will be needed. This situation is illustrated in figure 6-2 by line FG. The order placed in month 12, when the inventory was at level F, was expected to arrive in month 1. The order was a month late, arriving in month 2. Had there not been any safety stock, the organization would have run out of material when the inventory level crossed the dashed line representing the amount of safety stock.

Reorder Points

The inventory level that triggers the resupply process is called the reorder point. If everything were certain, then the reorder point would equal the normal usage during the normal lead time. But because of uncertainties in both usage and lead time, the reorder point (ROP) is equal to the safety stock (S) plus the normal demand during normal lead time (DNLT).

$$ROP = S + DNLT$$

In figure 6-2, the ROP illustrates a reorder point based on a safety stock of 129 units and an average demand over normal lead time of 237 units, or an ROP of 366 units. This means that whenever the inventory level gets down to 366, an order for the economic order quantity should be placed. On the average, the order will be received just as the inventory reaches 129 units, the safety stock. (See figure 6-5.)

Service Level Policy

The inventory manager who is willing to have five stock-outs every 100 order cycles is expressing a 95 percent service level. Arriving at such a service-level policy requires judging the cost of such a stock-out.

The cost of a stock-out is difficult to define. Will the stock-out result in a lost sale or, worse, a customer lost forever? What is the cost of customer ill will? What are the costs of rescheduling production due to a stock-out?

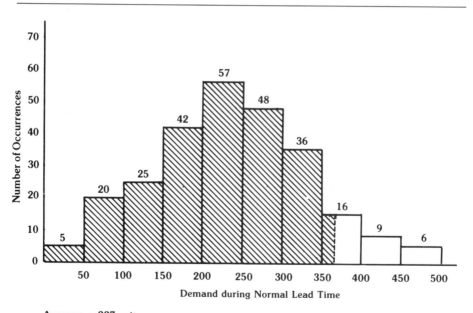

Average = 237 units
Sample = 264 occurrences
90% of Sample = 238 occurrences (shaded area)
90% Service = 366 units (interpolated)
Safety Stock = 366 units - 237 (normal usage) = 129 units

Figure 6-5. Safety Stock Determination
Based on Historical Demand

Once the stock-out cost has been estimated, then a safety-stock level can be set, based on the tradeoff between the estimated stock-out costs and the inventory carrying costs.

Computation of Safety Stocks

Assume the inventory manager decided on a 90 percent service level instead of a "safer" 95 percent level. This decision now must be translated into a safety-stock level. First, data on the demand during the normal lead time are collected. Next, a frequency diagram is drawn from which the average demand during normal lead time can be determined. Then, the stock level required to service 90 percent of the demands experienced in the past can be identified. Figure 6-5 illustrates this procedure, which provides the safety stock necessary to reduce the risk of stock-outs caused by above-average usage, as shown in figure 6-2, line HI.

Figure 6-5 uses the historical data without any assumptions regarding the distribution pattern of the demand. Often there are not as much data as used in this example (264 different periods); with less data, much the same result can be accomplished by assuming a normal distribution and calculating the mean and the standard deviation. Using standard tables for the normal distribution tells the user the number of standard deviations above the mean that will include 90 percent of expected demand during normal lead time. For a 90 percent service level, the proper number of standard deviations would be 1.28. Computing the standard deviation of the sample of historical data would permit establishing the safety stock. Assume the standard deviation were 98 units; the safety stock then would be 1.28 $\times$ 98 units, or 125 units. The reorder point would be the sum of the average usage during the normal lead time (237 units) plus the safety stock (125 units), or 362 units in total. This result is similar to the 129 units of safety stock based on the frequency diagram.

The computations of safety stock are equally applicable to both risks due to variable usage rates (as illustrated) and risks due to variations in lead time. In the case of safety stock for variable lead time, the number of days (weeks) beyond normal lead time that must be covered to give a desired service level must be determined. This can be achieved by the frequency-diagram approach, or it can be based on the normal distribution.

A conservative policy would add the safety stock based on usage variations to the safety stock based on lead-time variations. Since it is unlikely that excessive usage will occur at the same time as delays in deliveries, this policy results in more safety stock than required by the stated service-level policy. Since lead time often is controlled to some degree—for example, by expediting and follow-up procedures—the lead-time safety stocks might be reduced with less risk than the safety stocks due to demand fluctuations.

One-Time Order Quantities

In cases where items quickly become obsolete, the need will not remain long enough to require a reordering strategy. Unlike the previous models, this situation requires determining the best size of a single order. Imagine the problem faced by the newsboy; the apparel buyer estimating the order size of a seasonal, high-fashion item; or the grocery-store produce buyer. Each of these people must estimate the market and buy to cover a period of time: for the newsboy, it is the day's demand; for the apparel buyer, the season's demand; and for the produce buyer, the week's demand. The tradeoff they face is between not ordering enough, thus losing sales, versus ordering too much and having to throw the excess away or sell it at distress prices.

These situations lend themselves to classical marginal analysis. If the marginal profit (MP) of adding one more unit to the order is greater than the marginal loss (ML), then the order should be increased. The same logic applies in the uncertain case where one increases the order by one if the expected MP exceeds the expected ML. If P is the probability of selling the next unit, then the probability of not selling the next unit is 1-P. Therefore, the decision to add one to the order depends on whether or not:

$$P(MP) > = (1\text{-}P)(ML)$$

which simplifies to:

$$P> \ = \ \frac{(ML)}{(MP \ + \ ML)}$$

If one knows what the profit is when a sale is made and what the loss is if the sale is not made, it is an easy matter to compute the ratio ML/(ML + MP), assuming MP and ML remain constant over the relevant sales volumes. The decision maker will increase the order size until the probability of selling the unit to be added is less than the computed ratio.

For example:

Sale Price = $5.00   Unit Cost = $3.00
Therefore:
MP = (5-3) = $2.00   ML = $3.00
Computed Ratio = 3/(2 + 3) = .60

Nth Unit	Probability of Selling	
1	1.00	
2	.97	
3	.85	
4	.73	Optimum order size, since this is
5	.64	last item where P > = .60
6	.54	

7	.25
8	.05
9 or more	.00

Managing with "Zero" Inventory

The Japanese have provided a dramatic contrast to our buffering and decoupling uses of inventory. To the Japanese, inventory is wasteful and deters efficient operations. They take this position without ignoring any of the normal reasons for having inventory; the Japanese merely attack the reasons for having it, thus facilitating its reduction. This strategy allows their organizations to provide prompt service to customers without:

1. Investing large amounts in inventory

2. Consuming large amounts of warehouse and shop-floor space

3. Burying problems, such as defects, in piles of inventory

4. Doing extensive paperwork and follow-up to keep track of inventory

The Japanese approach often is referred to as the just-in-time concept. The goal is highly synchronized and dependable timing. Each operator should complete a unit just as the next person or operation requires that input. This eliminates work-in-process inventory much the same as in an assembly-line operation. This idea of a balanced flow is applied to as much of the transformation process as possible—from suppliers to finished goods.

Requirements of the Japanese Strategy

Because the just-in-time approach requires a predictable system, it is necessary that:

1. Interdependent groups cooperate.

2. Satisfactory quality units are supplied by vendors; there is no safety stock to draw from if a shipment is rejected.

3. Delivery is just in time because no safety stock is available.

4. Equipment performs reliably.

5. Employees are skilled so that dependable performance is assured.

6. Daily schedules are realistic.

Japan's major contribution lies not in the basic concepts but in the degree to which the ideas have been applied. Management concepts such as participative management, team building, and good communications are ingredients of group cooperation. Quality control, as manifested in the Japanese quality control circles, has enabled them to approach "zero defects." Preventive maintenance is the prime weapon in pursuit of dependable equipment performance. Continual emphasis on training and development of employee skills, along with programs designed to ingrain company values, has been effective in obtaining consistent labor inputs. Finally, meticulous planning and resistance to short-term changes help provide a stable production environment.

Kanban and Group Technology

Two techniques highlight the Japanese attack on work-in-process inventories. Both help to reduce the inventory required between sequential manufacturing operations.

The Kanban system is a simple, manual, card system that controls the manufacture of units. A limited number of Production Kanban cards and a similar number of Withdrawal Kanban cards are available. The number of cards represents the upper limit of inventory between work centers. Upon receipt of a Production Kanban (authorization to produce a specified number of units), a work center uses a Withdrawal Kanban to obtain a container of parts. The Withdrawal Kanban is placed with the container of parts and replaces the Production Kanban that had been placed with the container by the supplying work center. The replaced Production Kanban becomes an authorization to produce a new container of parts by the supplying work center. This process repeats itself all the way through the system until it reaches the outside vendors. In a very real sense, it is the final customer demand that pulls the work through the system, instead of queues of work orders pushing their way through from raw materials to finished goods.

Group technology is the other major means of achieving the low levels of inventory normally associated with assembly-line processes. This technique groups together equipment and operations that are common to a family of parts or products. This reduces the transit inventory that would exist if each operation were performed in a separate, functionally specialized department, thus reducing the lot size. To minimize inventory, the Japanese vigorously seek to reduce setup times, which are the economic driving force for large lots. Rapid changeovers have been achieved through the use of automation, preset tooling, and careful product, equipment, and tool design. This permits economic production of very small lots in the group-technology setting.

These two techniques, along with good general management practices, have allowed the Japanese to improve productivity and reduce inventory costs. They also allow the Japanese to underprice U.S. products in spite of the need to import most of their raw materials and then ship their products to our markets and in spite of tariff barriers. Over the past decade, U.S.

management has relied heavily upon the contributions of materials requirements planning (MRP), which has made significant contributions to the inventory issue and is consistent with Japanese techniques.

MRP and Inventory Management

MRP was introduced in chapter 4 in connection with planning and the master production schedule. The master production schedule represents customer orders in hand (firm orders) and anticipated, or forecast, orders that have been allocated to feasible time slots, or "buckets" in MRP language. These customer orders are referred to as "independent" demand since they are not controlled by the firm. The requirements that go into the manufacture of the end items represent derived demand and are referred to as "dependent" demand. The basic function of an MRP system is the translation of the independent demand into specific quantity and timing requirements for all dependent-demand items. In performing this function, MRP helps to answer the fundamental questions of inventory control—how much of what and when?

The Logic of MRP

The MRP program utilizes three types of information: (1) the master production schedule, (2) the current level of inventory, and (3) what goes into making the product. These data are found in the master production file, the stock status or inventory file, and the bill of materials file, respectively. The master production schedule gives the quantities and timing for end-product items to be produced. The inventory file provides information about stock on hand and on order and standard lead times. The bill of materials tells what goes into the product; furthermore, the sequence of manufacture is incorporated by structuring the list of components into levels. Level 0 is used for end items; levels 1, 2, and so on, are used to represent parts or subassemblies that go into higher level (lower number) parent items.

The MRP process starts with Level 0 by performing two steps: the first is called netting, and the second is called time phasing. The netting process amounts to checking for gross requirements over the planning horizon—say, six months—and reducing these gross requirements based on the amounts presently available from inventory. The result of the netting process is the net requirements in each time bucket over the planning period. Using the lead-time information, these net requirements are offset to an earlier time bucket where they represent planned-order releases. This is the time-phasing step.

Once netting and time phasing have been completed for all Level 0 items, the explosion process is performed. Here the planned-order releases are translated into gross requirements for all components that go into these planned orders. The bill of materials is used to perform this step. Following the explosion process, the procedure advances to the next lower level—say, Level 1—and repeats the netting, time-phasing, and exploding steps. This continues until the planned orders have been identified for the lowest-level items in the bill of materials.

Consider the example in figure 6-6: the master production schedule (fig. 6-6a) reflects the demand for a particular style of picture frame. The bill of materials (fig. 6-6b) indicates that each frame consists of a frame, two backing sheets, and a piece of glass cut from a larger sheet. The process calls for cutting the glass, followed by an assembly operation. Inventory file data are summarized in figure 6-6c. The netting and time phasing are shown in the MRP table (fig. 6-6d). The explosion of the planned assembly orders is shown in the MRP table for the backing sheets (fig. 6-6e).

Lot Sizing in MRP

The dependent demand aspect of MRP leads to what is called lumpy demand. It is this lumpy-demand characteristic that makes EOQ and related techniques difficult or inappropriate to apply below the 0, or end-item, level. Figure 6-7 shows the contrast between the uniform usage appropriate for EOQ and the lumpy demand to which MRP is more appropriate. In the picture-frame example, the EOQ for backings might have been 500 units. Therefore, when the net requirement for 350 units was encountered, an order for 500 units would have been placed. The excess 150 units might remain in stock for a long time, possibly until they became obsolete.

Even at the highest level, demand may not be uniform enough to apply the standard EOQ approach. In order of increasing complexity, the following approaches become less sensitive to the standard EOQ assumptions:

1. Period order quantity—converts the EOQ into the economic number of months to cover with each order

2. Part-period balancing—an incremental approach that adds additional months' requirements to an order until the carrying cost equals the ordering cost

3. Wagner-Whitin Algorithm—an application of dynamic programming to inventory requirements over a specified planning period

Below the top level, the simple lot-for-lot approach is favored. This approach avoids the small residual stocks that are of little value, and, if it errs, it does so in the low inventory direction.

Item: Frames	Time Bucket (Weeks)					
	1	2	3	4	5	6
MPS Requirements: Frames	100		250		175	

Figure 6-6a.   Master Production Schedule

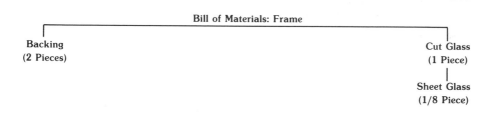

Figure 6-6b.   Bill of Materials

Inventory Data

Item	On Hand	On Order	Normal Lead Time
Frames	350	None	2 Weeks
Backing	None	None	1 Week
Cut Glass	None	None	1 Week
Sheet Glass	500	None	8 Weeks

Figure 6-6c.   Inventory File Data

Item: Frame	Time Bucket (Weeks)					
	1	2	3	4	5	6
Gross Requirements	100		250		175	
On Hand & On Order	250	250	0	0	neg	
Net Requirements	0	0	0	0	175	
Planned Orders			175			

Figure 6-6d.   MRP Table for Frame

Item: Backing			Time Bucket (Weeks)			
	1	2	3	4	5	6
Gross Requirements			350			
On Hand & On Order	0	0	neg	0		
Net Requirements	0	0	350	0		
Planned Orders		350				

Figure 6-6e. MRP Table for Backing

Safety Stock and Safety Lead Time in MRP

MRP advocates discourage the use of safety stocks for dependent demand items. One of the goals is to reduce inventory and fractional lots of safety stock that will not support a full production run. Safety stock can serve as a protection against variations in quantity—for example, scrap losses or short shipments. Safety lead time, in the sense of producing or bringing in a complete lot size early, is a hedge against timing problems, such as those caused by late deliveries or production delays. The Japanese approach would also discourage safety stock as well as safety time. The emphasis is on reducing the causes that lead to safety stocks, such as breakdowns, defective products, or production capacity expended on the wrong jobs due to invalid job priorities. If safety stock or safety lead times are used, those stocks should be made very clear to all so that priorities are not distorted. Generally, the firm should not be expediting a job to replace safety stock at the expense of efforts on jobs going to a customer.

Summary of MRP Benefits and Limitations

MRP makes a major contribution to the planning and acquisition of materials. In the short term, it tests the feasibility of the master production schedule when the component schedules and purchases are reviewed against available capacity and vendor lead times. MRP allows establishment of the valid priority of jobs, by highlighting which items should be expedited due to overdue situations and which items should be de-expedited due to decisions to delay orders. In the long term, MRP is useful in estimating capacity requirements through translating long-range market forecasts into specific capacity requirements.

The major limitations of MRP are associated with its demands for accurate data and extensive computer capacity. Since minimum inventory is one of the selling features of MRP, the system depends on the inventory records being very accurate (98 percent or better). Furthermore, if the bill

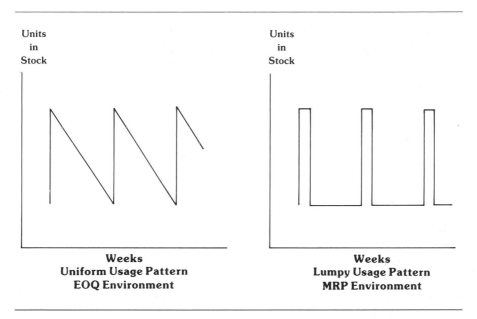

Figure 6-7.   Contrast between Uniform and
Lumpy Demands on Inventory

of materials is not current and accurate, MRP will translate higher-level demand into incorrect lower-level requirements. This could result in work stoppages, quality problems, or wasted material. Therefore, it is imperative to
maintain accurate stock-status records and closely manage engineering
changes that affect the bill of materials. Many organizations have failed to
achieve the accuracy levels required, with resulting failure of the MRP system.
The volume of computations mandates the use of a computer, which brings
many changes into organizations that are not computerized. Even with computer facilities, major changes in inventory and engineering procedures may
be required.

Finally, MRP is not equally applicable to all organizations. Since it derives
its value from coordinating the assembly of many components into a final
product in batches, the technique applies best to assembly and batch manufacturing of multi-part products. On the other hand, fabricators often are
dealing with one component, which negates MRP's strength, and process
industries are less batch oriented, which devalues the replanning capability
of MRP.

Physical Care of Inventories

This section discusses two of the major issues associated with the physical
control and care of inventory—storage methods and record keeping.

Warehousing and Stock-keeping Objectives

The objective of warehousing (stock keeping) is to store stock-keeping units (SKUs) at minimum cost. This goal requires efficient use of space, elimination of unnecessary rehandling, protection of the goods, avoidance of obsolescence, and prompt delivery of the goods to users when requested.

Storage Methods

The storage of materials involves physically holding the inventory, handling it into and out of storage, and efficiently locating items into and out of storage areas. There are many ways to store materials physically, each with advantages and disadvantages.

Containerized inventory can be mass stored on open floor space, one container stacked on another in rows. This provides dense storage (high space utilization) but results in a great deal of rehandling and possibly misplacing material behind stacks of inventory. Shelves or pallet racks can improve accessibility. In this case, every unit can be obtained directly, with lower rehandling cost and damage. Racks and shelves often require more space than mass storage to accommodate the same volume of material.

The methods of locating inventory can vary—from relying on people's memory to checking addresses maintained in computer files. Each SKU can be assigned a specific location (e.g., 1/2 hp. motors may be assigned to Aisle 12, Rack J, Shelf 3, Position B). Such addressing schemes provide precise locations. Unfortunately, they lead to low space utilization (half empty on the average) and problems in reorganization when inventory volume grows.

Random storage circumvents these space problems by storing items where there is space, not necessarily with similar goods. The challenge here is dealing with record-keeping errors and excessive order-picking costs. These are potential drawbacks to the random-locating approach, but the computer has helped significantly. For example, the computer can analyze order picking so that the stockkeeper is directed to find items in sequence of their position in the stockroom. One trip through the stockroom is required instead of a back-and-forth procedure. Computerization in stock keeping has been extended to automatic storage and retrieval systems that will take stock to a storage location, store the items, and update the computerized inventory locator file. Withdrawals from stock are similarly automated and driven by pick lists, which also can be computer generated.

Finally, the just-in-time philosophy has led to the concept of wall-to-wall inventory. This concept focuses on bringing raw material directly to the point of use in a plant. As a product flows through the plant, parts are added until completion. Minimum stocks are held on the factory floor. Formal stockrooms are reduced or eliminated. This contrasts sharply with the locked and controlled stockrooms used with many MRP systems as a means of assuring the necessary accuracy of inventory counts.

Record-keeping Requirements

The use of random storage procedures requires accurate records. The inventory manager must be able to specify the location and quantities available for any SKU. Records must be kept on: shipments received and storage locations, withdrawals from stock, transfers of material between departments, shipments from finished goods, and write-offs due to scrap, damage, or obsolescence.

Accurate records of inventory transactions are a necessity. Errors lead to wasted time looking for material, production shutdowns due to stock-outs, and inaccuracies in the MRP system, scheduling, and purchasing operations. The importance of inventory records justifies extensive efforts to detect and eliminate errors. The cost of physically counting every warehoused item one or more times per year is substantial, and errors are possible. Many firms are eliminating the annual physical inventory in favor of cycle counting.

Cycle counting audits inventory records throughout the year. This catches errors earlier and reduces the expense of the concentrated annual physical inventory. The cycle count of a specific item may be scheduled just before a resupply shipment is expected, when the stock is lowest and there are fewer items to count. Highly active items are counted more frequently than slow-moving items; the more activity an item undergoes, the more likely that errors will occur.

Locked (closed) stockrooms reduce unauthorized withdrawals of materials. Record keeping is under the control of a trained stockkeeper. To reduce human errors, more recording tasks can be diverted to the computer. Computer-generated pick cards, prepunched with the quantity to be withdrawn, reduce the recording errors. Once the order is picked, the prepunched withdrawal card is submitted to the computer. Only exceptions, such as partially filled orders, will require stockkeeper inputs.

References

Chase, Richard B., and Aquilano, Nicholas J. *Production and Operations Management.* 4th ed. Homewood, IL: Richard D. Irwin, 1985.

Fogarty, Donald W., and Hoffmann, Thomas R. *Production and Inventory Management.* Cincinnati, OH: South-Western Publishing Co., 1983.

Hall, Robert W. *Zero Inventories.* Homewood, IL: Dow Jones-Irwin, 1983.

Levin, Richard I.; Kirkpatrick, Charles A.; and Rubin, David S. *Quantitative Approaches to Management.* 5th ed. New York: McGraw-Hill, 1982.

Orlicky, Joseph. *Material Requirements Planning: The New Way of Life in Production and Inventory Management.* New York: McGraw-Hill, 1975.

Pascale, Richard Tanner, and Athos, Anthony G. *The Art of Japanese Management.* New York: Simon & Schuster, 1981.

Discussion Questions

1. What is meant by the decoupling function of inventories?

2. Discuss the cost trade-offs that are reflected in the EOQ and ELS formulas.

3. What happens to the ELS formula if (p) becomes very large relative to (d)? What if (d) = (p)? What real-world interpretations can you give to these outcomes?

4. What are the assumptions of the traditional EOQ formula?

5. Describe the procedure for finding the best order quantity when price breaks are available.

6. How does the approach to one-time purchases differ from repetitive purchase items?

7. How do Kanban, group technology, and wall-to-wall inventories contribute to the goal of zero inventories?

8. Under what circumstances is MRP most applicable, and what are some of the prerequisites for a successful MRP system?

9. Discuss the pros and cons of different methods of storing goods.

10. Describe the concept of cycle counting, and indicate its advantages relative to traditional annual physical inventories.

Problems

1. Your company is offered the following price breaks on an electrical component of which it buys 1,000 per year.

Quantity	Price
0-200 pcs.	$12.50 each
201 & up	$10.00 each

Your company has determined that it costs 10 percent of the purchase unit price to store an item a year. Furthermore, your ordering costs amount to $15 per order. What is your best order quantity? Do not overlook the savings in overall purchase cost (the last term in the total-cost equation).

2. Given the following data on the 12 items your shop stocks, which ones should receive very tight control, moderate control, and loose control?

Item	Annual Volume	Unit Value	Item	Annual Volume	Unit Value
D322	3,000	25.00	X563	1,000	5.00
Y791	20,000	.50	M749	10,000	.25
B555	1,750	100.00	Z345	30,000	.25
A658	10,000	5.00	Z664	10,000	2.00
T832	1,000	1.25	R779	1,400,000	.10
K842	1,000	3.75	L335	5,000	2.00

3. Develop the time-phased inventory records (similar to figures 6-6d and 6-6e) for items A, B, C, and D, based on the data provided.

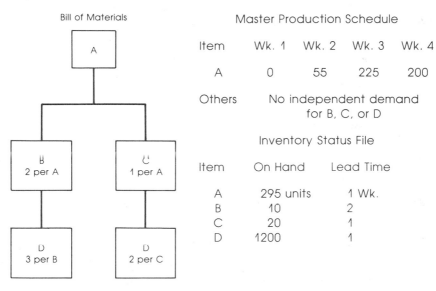

Bill of Materials

Master Production Schedule

Item	Wk. 1	Wk. 2	Wk. 3	Wk. 4
A	0	55	225	200

Others   No independent demand for B, C, or D

Inventory Status File

Item	On Hand	Lead Time
A	295 units	1 Wk.
B	10	2
C	20	1
D	1200	1

Chapter 7

Quality Control

The manager who says, "The objective of our company is to produce the highest-quality product at the lowest possible cost" does not understand the role of quality in a business firm. Chances are, *neither* the highest-quality product *nor* the lowest-cost product is the appropriate goal. Rather, some balance between quality and cost should be sought. Quality is expensive, and higher quality generally can be achieved only by spending more money and increasing the unit cost of the product. If the customer is willing to pay a higher price for better quality, then a high-quality strategy may be effective. But if additional increases in quality force the price too high, the firm will price itself (or "quality itself") right out of the market.

The relevant question is: How much quality do we want and at what cost/price? A Rolls Royce presumably has higher quality than a Volkswagen, yet it would be difficult to say which is the better buy from a quality standpoint, due to the relationship between quality and price.

To better understand quality in the production of goods and services, we must determine what quality is—and what it is not, what the relevant costs of quality are, and how quality is produced or controlled. Furthermore, we should appreciate the importance of quality in products and services as more than just an economic concept. It has strong legal and social implications as well. It is inconvenient to buy an electrical appliance that doesn't work, but if things such as automobiles or health care are of poor quality, lives may be lost.

Many people equate "quality" with luxurious products or lavish services. Expensive sports cars, grand hotels, exclusive clubs and restaurants, fur coats, and precious jewelry are typical examples of "quality" goods and services. In truth, each may have high or low quality relative to its price, just as simpler items have varying degrees of quality.

Product and Service Quality

Much of the following discussion concerns manufactured products, since many of the pertinent quality techniques have been developed within and for manufacturing. Service firms recognize, however, that quality is no less important to their success and that many of the tools developed for products can be applied to services as well. The concepts and tools must be adapted, of course, to fit the different nature of services and the process of service delivery.

As the chapter unfolds, consider how each topic may be applied to a service business, such as a bank, hospital, university, or insurance company. "Products" become checking accounts, surgical operations, undergraduate courses, and insurance policies. "Defects" may be translated into "errors;" "transportation" becomes "delivery of the service;" and so on. Not every concept will apply, but most will.

Many service firms produce a product as well as a service. In a pizza parlor, for example, the quality of the food and the quality of the service can be separated; one can be excellent while the other is poor, and either can change from time to time. With firms that are more exclusively service oriented, defining the unit of output becomes difficult; legal counseling, consulting, teaching, and many government operations, such as parks and recreation or national defense, are examples. The closer the firm is to a pure service organization, the more difficult it is to define, measure, and control quality.

New methods are being developed, however, to measure quality characteristics and to identify countable errors in service industries. As these efforts continue, the establishment and use of quality-enhancement programs in service-oriented organizations are likely to increase as well.

The Meaning of Quality

To grasp the meaning of quality and its control, consider a business: Quality Doghouses, Inc. The basic product, a doghouse, is made from plywood and is spray painted. The deluxe model has a shingle roof, carpeting, and a chain that attaches to a clip next to a swinging door. The price of the deluxe model is twice the price of the standard model, but the deluxe model is not necessarily the "high-quality" model. Either model can be high or low quality.

Quality Defined

Quality is a characteristic of a product, as is its size, shape, or composition. Specifically, it is a characteristic that determines its value in the market and how well it will perform the function for which it was designed. The quality of a product in general is expressed as a standard, and the quality of specific units of that product is measured in terms of the degree of conformance with the standard.

Thus, the definition of quality must include both the standard and conformance to the standard. Merely changing the standard does not change quality; quality must actually be built into the manufacture of a product or the provision of a service.

The standard may be set in a number of ways, First, customers may set standards by their past buying behavior; market research gives some idea of the quality level customers want and are willing to pay for. Second, top management may set a standard in terms of the policy or strategy the firm wants to implement; it can aim at the top, bottom, or middle of the quality market. Third, a design technician in the firm may set a tolerance that a certain part must meet if it is to fit properly with other parts. Ultimately, each of these standards must be translated into specific technical standards to guide the manufacture and assembly of the product.

These concepts can be illustrated with the doghouse example. The primary function of the doghouse is to protect Fido from the weather. To achieve this, the roof must not leak; this standard will be applied in a "leak test" as part of the manufacturing process. Another aspect of the doghouse is the finish. Runs in the paint will not affect the function of the doghouse, but they may affect its value in the market if the doghouse buyer considers it important. Another standard must be developed for the number and type of tolerable blemishes in the paint.

In manufacturing a product, the following fundamental elements of control must be applied to the quality dimensions of the product:

1. Measure the quality characteristic.

2. Compare actual results to the standard.

3. Take corrective action when the deviation between actual results and the standard exceeds tolerable limits.

Corrective action may consist of stopping the process, retraining workers, using different materials, or rejecting the day's production.

Dimensions of Quality

Quality is not a single characteristic; it is multidimensional. Some organizations may separate some of these dimensions from their definition of quality, but they are related so closely that they should be included as part of the total quality concept.

1. Functionality. This refers to whether the product performs its function at the end of the manufacturing process or when it is first put to use. Functionality can be measured on a yes-or-no basis—either the light

bulb works or it doesn't—or as a continuous measure—in terms of how many foot candles of light the bulb emits.

2. Reliability. How long will the product function under normal conditions? A product may function perfectly the first time but fail before completing its normal life span.

3. Durability. How well and how long will the product function under adverse conditions? Can the product withstand shock, vibration, heat, cold, dust, and other conditions that it reasonably might be expected to encounter?

4. Esthetic characteristics. This refers to the appearance of the product and is not necessarily related to its function. The smoothness of the surface, the symmetry of decorative designs, and the absence of chips, dents, or scratches illustrate this dimension.

5. Safety. Will the product perform its function without unnecessarily endangering the user? Electrical appliances should not produce electrical shocks during normal use; lawnmower blades should stay attached to the spindle.

A high-quality doghouse cannot be produced unless all these aspects have been considered.

Total Quality Control

The quality-control function in an organization often is viewed as sort of a police department that checks outgoing products and gives tickets to offenders. A total quality program, however, must include much more than just an inspection function. Quality cannot be *inspected* into a product: it must be *designed* and *built* into the product. And quality control assures that this has been done.

There are several areas within the firm where quality (good or bad) can be introduced into the product.

Product Design

The end product probably will be no better than the design that preceded it. Design engineers must consider not only the functionality of the early prototypes but also the ease with which the elements of the product can be produced in quantity and assembled into final units. The choices of screws versus rivets, tongue-and-groove versus miter joints, and braces or no braces all will determine whether the product will withstand the quality tests of the consumer. Designers may have to revise their basic design several times to fit the needs and constraints of later stages of development and manufacture.

Process Design

To manufacture the doghouse, certain machines, such as saws, sanders, spray painters, and hand tools, are needed. The choice of machines will affect the quality of output; more expensive saws may make a cleaner cut and give a closer fit of parts in final assembly.

The effect of other aspects of process design on quality is less obvious but nonetheless important. The layout employed, materials handling and storage methods used, sequencing of operations, and even maintenance policies can influence the number of defective units produced.

Raw Materials

Generally, the better the quality of the raw materials, the better the quality of the finished product. Plywood, for example, comes in several grades, which indicate the smoothness of the surface. Cheaper grades of wood could be used, but, to maintain the standard, much of the material would have to be filled, sanded, or discarded. Purchased parts, such as hinges or chains, also must meet specifications, even though the firm does not manufacture these items.

The problem of obtaining raw materials of proper quality can be subdivided into several steps. First, the proper material must be selected. Should it be plywood, particle board, or masonite? Second, the appropriate vendor must be selected. Third, incoming raw material receipts should be monitored to assure that the quality standard is met throughout the manufacturing period. Failure to consider any of these three steps may jeopardize the quality of the end product.

Employees

In addition to materials and equipment, the third major input category is people. To achieve the quality goals, employees must be trained properly in the quality aspects of the task they are to perform, and they must be motivated to produce at the level of desired quality. Selection and training policies should consider the level of quality that workers are expected to achieve. It is incorrect to assume that workers naturally will produce at the right quality level. And it is unwise, and often costly, to rely on inspection to police the employees' work.

Operation of the Production Process

The doghouse manufacturer might have the best design, the best equipment, the best raw materials, and the best employees, but if it fails to *manage* the quality function in its day-by-day operations, it still may not produce an acceptable product. The maintenance policy for equipment may be sound but not implemented carefully. Housekeeping could be lax and damage the product during manufacturing. Supervisory styles, communications, scheduling, stores control, wage and salary policies, and many other operating policies, rules, and procedures can determine whether the firm produces at or below its quality capability. Seemingly insignificant decisions, such as the scheduling of coffee breaks, often can have a pronounced impact on quality.

Packaging

Many firms incorrectly assume that their quality responsibilities end when the item comes off the assembly line. If it passes "final inspection," then a quality product has been produced. The customer, however, really does the *final* inspection. If a product fails to meet the customer's quality criteria when it is put to use, then it is a defective unit. Packaging is the first of several activities between the assembly line and the point of purchase that can influence the quality of the product.

If the doghouse is sent out with no packaging at all, it will end up with scratches, dents, parts missing, and a variety of other defects unacceptable to the customer. It could be put in a plastic bag to protect it from dirt or in a cardboard box to reduce the effects of rough handling. Ultimately, the firm could construct a packing crate more costly than the doghouse itself to assure that the item arrives in the same condition as it left the plant. Packaging that is cost-effective and commensurate with the characteristics of the product must be selected.

Transporting

Among the alternatives for shipping the doghouse to market are truck, air, rail, or boat. The type of transportation chosen will influence not only the costs but also the quality of the product. Air cargo is subject to extreme pressure and temperature changes. Rail and truck shipments may involve vibration and exposure to the weather, as well as several loading and unloading operations. Company-owned vehicles may be specifically adapted to the size and weight of the cargo, but cost-effectiveness also must be considered.

Obviously, the packaging used and the transportation method chosen are interdependent. Items shipped by commercial carrier may need more protection, but air shipments should minimize the package-weight required. Whatever combination of packaging and transportation is chosen, the decision should be tempered by the effect on the quality of the product and should fit with the firm's overall quality policy.

Storage

An area often overlooked as a quality determinant is storage. The doghouses will be kept in warehouses, stockrooms, and other storage facilities for weeks, months, or years before they are sold. The product is fairly durable, but there are limits to how high it should be stacked, how far it can be dropped, and what environmental conditions it can withstand. A more delicate product might have severe restrictions on allowable temperature, humidity, dust, or light. Perishable products with a "shelf life" should be rotated to assure freshness.

Packaging also is interdependent with storing: the more protective the packaging, the less likely the product is to deteriorate during storage. Also, packaging materials can be marked with storing instructions that help assure that the product will be in an acceptable condition when needed.

After all the effort that has been put into the design and manufacture of a quality product, it would be unfortunate to lose it through careless storage and handling.

A Total Quality-control Program

A total quality-control (TQC) approach recognizes quality as a top business priority and coordinates all activities toward this goal. TQC makes quality a part of everyone's job and emphasizes prevention rather than detection and correction.

Many organizations are developing various TQC approaches, and most are demonstrating impressive records of success. Ford Motor Company is one example. According to Ford's executive director of quality assurance, quality is up 59 percent in automobiles and 47 percent in trucks over 1980 levels. The Ford approach to TQC is based on the following elements:

1. Employee awareness and commitment—Employees must understand the importance of quality and have the proper tools and information to achieve quality targets.

2. Teamwork—Managers in all areas promote communication and cooperation in an effort to enhance quality.

3. Quality designed into the product—The design can be mass produced to meet customer specifications and expectations.

4. Quality built into the product—The production process is managed day-by-day to assure that the desired quality level is maintained.

5. Quality monitored and customers served—An ongoing flow of information is maintained to assure quick response to problems and to prevent their reoccurrence.

6. Quality improvement in outside suppliers—By working more closely with carefully selected suppliers, the company is able to obtain quality raw materials and purchased parts.

In daily operations, these six elements guide decisions and actions that affect quality. Improved quality leads, in turn, to improved productivity, cost control, and profits.

Factors Affecting Quality

A total quality-control (TQC) approach requires an understanding of the stages of production where quality is affected: product and service design, process design, raw materials, and so on. If TQC is to lead to improved quality, however, managers also must understand the organizational factors that influence quality levels. Figure 7-1 is a useful conceptual framework for organizing these factors. Furthermore, it shows that inspection and testing do not improve the quality level. They can only catch some defects before they reach the customer and provide information to managers about problems that need correction.

Behavioral and Technical Factors Affecting Quality

The actual quality of the product or service when it reaches the customer is determined by a multitude of factors involved in the creation and delivery of the output. Generally, these can be divided into behavioral factors (those that relate to the people in the process) and technical factors (the characteristics of the tools, equipment, materials, and processes).

Some behavioral factors, such as the amount of training an employee has received, will determine the potential for achieving high quality. A poorly trained employee simply is not as capable of high-quality work as a well-trained one. Similarly, technical factors, such as the capabilities of the equipment or the specifications of the raw material, determine the potential quality level of the process.

On the other hand, some behavioral and technical factors influence the quality levels in day-to-day operations. That is, they determine whether or not the potential quality level of the process is achieved. For example, an employee may be properly trained and capable of doing high-quality work, but if he or she is poorly motivated due to inadequate rewards, this individual may fail to work up to his or her quality potential. Similarly, machines that are poorly maintained or materials that are handled improperly can introduce defects into a process that has been well designed but badly managed. If quality expectations are not being met, management must determine the reason(s) and attempt to isolate the specific problem. Obviously, it would make no sense to try to increase employees' motivation toward higher quality

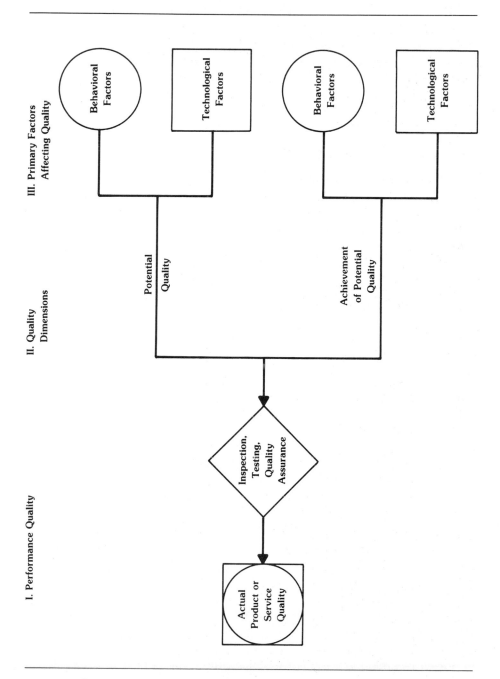

Figure 7-1.   Behavioral and Technical Factors Affecting Quality

if employees already are doing their best with the poor tools and materials with which they have to work. On the other hand, it is useless to invest in better equipment if employees lack the motivation to produce proper levels of quality.

Quality Circles

A popular topic in American business today is the phenomenon of quality circles. Originally intended as a means of improving product quality, quality circles have become human-relations tools that can affect quality, cost, the quality of work life, and the satisfaction and morale of the work force. The primary results of quality circles indicate, however, that quality can be influenced by everyone, not just the quality inspector.

In Japan after World War II, the urgent goal was to rebuild. Japan achieved its immediate objective by manufacturing cheap, low-quality goods and exporting them throughout the world. In the 1950s, "made in Japan" meant cheap junk. A program to raise the quality of manufactured products was launched, and today Japan is among the world's leading producers of high-quality sophisticated electronic and mechanical products. Much of that transition is due to quality circles.

A quality circle is a group of workers who meet together weekly to discuss problems of quality, or other factors, and develop solutions. Employees who are close to the work on a daily basis often can find answers not apparent to engineers and analysts. If possible, solutions are implemented immediately, and the result is a higher-quality product and workers who feel they have made a positive contribution to that product.

Quality circles are no longer unique to Japan. American companies such as Westinghouse, Techtronics, Motorola, and many others have reported excellent results. Quality circles also have been successfully implemented in government operations such as the Naval Shipyard at Norfolk, Virginia. Based upon past results, the potential for quality improvement in products and services through the implementation of quality circles is enormous.

Cost Considerations

Earlier, we referred to the costs of quality. That relationship can be explained with a format similar to that used for the EOQ formula (chapter 6), although in this instance the costs are not as well defined. In quality analysis, the same balancing of opposing costs is used but without the benefit of a formula to solve the problem.

The firm wants to select a quality program that puts the proper emphasis on quality—not too much and not too little. Figure 7-2 illustrates this concept. With little emphasis on quality, the costs associated with quality effort will be minimal, but the costs associated with poor quality output will be high. If too much emphasis is placed on quality, the reverse will be true. The optimal quality program, measured by the minimum of the sum of these costs, is likely to be somewhere between these extremes.

Costs associated with quality effort include those related to:

1.   Better design

2.   Better equipment and process design

3.   Better raw materials

4.   Better trained or more skilled workers

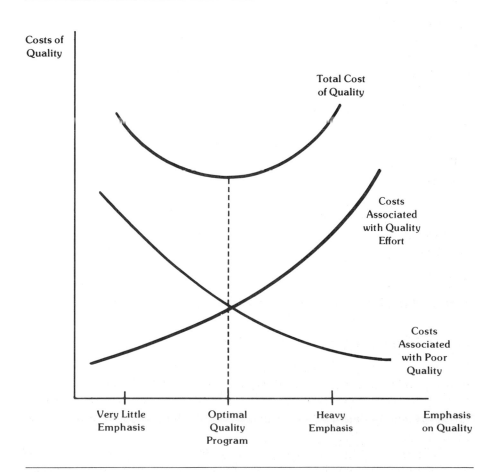

Figure 7-2.   Quality-Cost Relationships

5. More motivated workers

6. More careful processing

7. More effective inspection

8. More emphasis on post-processing activities of packaging, storing, and shipping

As these costs rise, with greater emphasis, the costs associated with poor quality output fall. The latter costs include those from:

1. Poor company reputation

2. Lower sales

3. More returns and complaints

4. More repairs and adjustments

5. More scrap and rework

6. Lower employee morale

7. More lawsuits, fines, and penalties

8. Higher manufacturing (unit) cost

The optimal quality program will be different for each industry (for example, pharmaceuticals versus dog food) and may vary among firms within an industry (Cadillac versus Chevrolet). Cost accounting methods do not yet permit a precise solution to the optimal quality problem; educated judgment is the only available method.

Statistical Quality Control

As indicated, a total quality program involves much more than simply inspecting the product, yet applications of statistical quality control to inspection and testing can be the key to *assuring* that the quality program meets its goals. In fact, many firms have dropped the term "quality control" in favor of a more descriptive term, such as quality assurance, quality evaluation, customer assurance, or product integrity.

Inspection and testing can be casual or sophisticated. Some items can be inspected visually by the worker or an inspector to assure that no parts are missing and that the product "looks okay." In other applications, such as in pharmaceuticals, elaborate tests are employed against rigid standards for purity, weight, and content. Inspection points sometimes are placed throughout the process to monitor progress at each stage of completion. In still other instances, only a final inspection is performed.

Some defects are dichotomous; that is, the item is either good or bad. For example, a light bulb either lights or doesn't, and a packet of washers contains the right number of units or it doesn't. This situation is referred to as quality by attributes.

In other instances, quality can be measured by some continuous gauge. A can of coffee rarely contains *exactly* one pound. An acceptable range for this measure might be 15.5 to 17.0 ounces; a container with less than 15.5 ounces or more than 17.0 ounces is considered a "defective" unit. Other examples would be the diameter of a rod, the temperature of a mixture, or the percent of fat in hamburger. Quality in these cases is measured by variables.

Inspection and testing are performed for two basic reasons: (1) to remove all or most of the defective items, which is done by 100 percent inspection or "screening," and (2) to predict the number of defects present, in which a small sample of items is checked by acceptance sampling.

Screening

Screening is performed when the cost from a defect is relatively high and the cost of inspection is relatively low. Screening also is indicated when many defects are believed present.

Consider a simple test for an electronic part that goes into a TV set. The test costs an average of 80¢ per unit for the inspector's time, equipment, supplies, and overhead. If a bad part is assembled into the set, the set will not work and will be rejected by the final inspection at the end of the assembly line. Rejected sets then are examined by a technician who must find the problem, remove the bad part, and replace it with a good part. This procedure costs the company $20 for each defective set.

If only 3 percent of the parts are defective, then 3 percent of the assembled TV sets will incur the $20 repair cost, or an average of 60¢ per set. But inspecting every part increases the cost of each set by 80¢. In this instance, the firm would not perform the test because it would be more economical to repair the sets after assembly. If however, 5 percent of the parts were bad, it would pay to do the inspection. The 80¢ inspection cost per unit would be lower than the average repair cost of 5 percent times $20, or $1 per set. The indifference point is 4 percent, where the cost of inspection and the cost of repair would be the same.

The same analysis can be applied to defective items that reach the customer, but the costs usually are not as well defined. Defects that reach the customer cost the firm in return, repair, customer dissatisfaction, and, occasionally, lawsuits. These costs must be balanced against the costs of testing and inspection before the product is sold.

One hundred percent inspection or screening does not guarantee freedom from defects; no inspection is perfect. Items can be inspected three, four, or even ten times and still malfunction. The defect may not show up in the test. It may have been overlooked, or it may have been introduced between the time of inspection and use of the product.

Acceptance Sampling

Acceptance sampling applies statistical analysis to a small sample of items to predict the number of defects present. It can be divided into the major categories of batch sampling and process sampling.

Batch sampling by attributes. Suppose the electronic parts mentioned above were purchased from a supplier in lots of 1,000 units. If the batch contained 4 percent or less defects, the firm would want to accept it and use it in production. If it contained 5 percent or more defects, it would be best to reject it and either return it to the manufacturer or screen the batch before use. The challenge is to predict the number of defects in the batch through statistical analysis of a sample.

If a firm is sampling by attributes (the part is either good or bad), a sample is drawn, the number of defects in the sample is counted, and then the lot is accepted or rejected based upon the results of the sample.

A sample plan contains two elements: a sample size and an acceptance number. Charts and tables are available for determining the proper sample plan, but to use these effectively, the underlying theory of sampling must be understood.

For example, take a sample of 50 units, with an acceptance number of two. This plan says to count the number of defects in the sample and accept the lot if there are zero, one, or two defects; three or more defects in the sample would indicate the lot should be rejected. Since sampling does not give perfect information; there are two types of errors, as illustrated in figure 7-3.

In the example, a "good lot" is one with 4 percent or less defects; a "bad lot" is one with more than 4 percent defective items. With a sample of 50, it would be possible to get three or more defective items even though the lot contains less then 4 percent defective (less than 40 out of 1,000). The sample then would indicate rejection of the lot, which would be a Type I error. Usually, however, the sample would be correct, and the lot would be accepted.

With probability theory, the chance of accepting or rejecting a lot with a given percent defective can be calculated. Calculating the probability of acceptance for each different lot percent defective produces an operating-characteristics curve like the one in figure 7-4.

The operating-characteristics curve indicates that lots with 2 percent defective items will be accepted 85 percent of the time; 15 percent of the

	Accept	Reject
Good Lot	No Error	Type I Error (Alpha)
Bad Lot	Type II Error (Beta)	No Error

Figure 7-3. Sampling Errors

time they will be rejected. This 15 percent is α (alpha) and often is called the "producer's risk," because even though a good lot was produced, by chance it was rejected. Similarly, a lot with 7 percent defective would, with this sample plan, be accepted 20 percent of the time. This probability is labeled β (beta) and is called the "consumer's risk," because the consumer runs a 20 percent chance of accepting this lot that really should be rejected.

A sample plan is set by choosing values for four variables. First is the specification, in terms of percent defective, of a really good lot, one that very often should be accepted. The percent defective specified is called the acceptable quality level (AQL), and the probability associated with "very often" is alpha. In this example, lots with an AQL of 2 percent will be accepted 85 percent of the time, but the plan will reject them 15 percent of the time. Next, a really bad lot, one that should be accepted infrequently, must be specified. The bad lot percent defective is called the lot tolerance percent defective (LTPD), and it is accepted with a probability of 20 percent (beta). These four coordinates define one, and only one, operating-characteristics curve that is associated with only one sample plan made up of a sample size and a given acceptance number.

To make fewer errors, or if the firm is willing to make more errors, a different sample plan must be used. The problem is one of balancing a Type I error (alpha) against a Type II error (beta) and then balancing the cost of these errors against the cost of sampling. Figure 7-5 illustrates the relationship of the acceptance number to the types of errors when the sample size remains the same. A "tighter" plan (n, sample size = 50; c, acceptance number = 1) will make more Type I errors but fewer Type II errors. Fewer lots of any percent defective will be accepted, meaning that more good lots will be

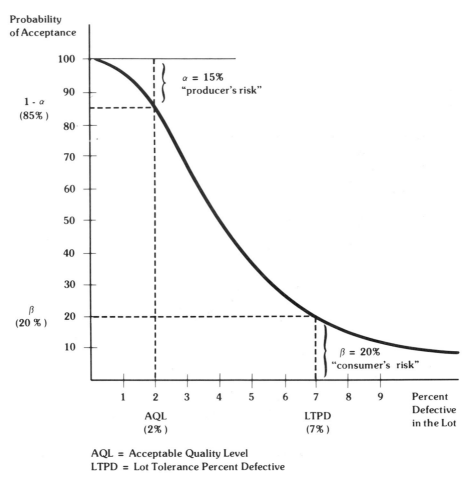

Figure 7-4.   Operating-Characteristics Curve

rejected but fewer bad ones will be accepted. A "looser" sample plan (n = 50; c = 3) would do the opposite.

To make fewer errors of both types, the firm must go to a larger, more accurate sample. Figure 7-6 illustrates the effect of a larger sample size using the same relative acceptance number. The larger sample will lead to fewer errors but will be more costly.

The operating-characteristics curve illustrates the theory behind batch sampling for attributes. To find an appropriate sample plan, however, the decision maker needs only to set levels for the AQL, LTPD, alpha, and beta and use the charts established for this purpose.

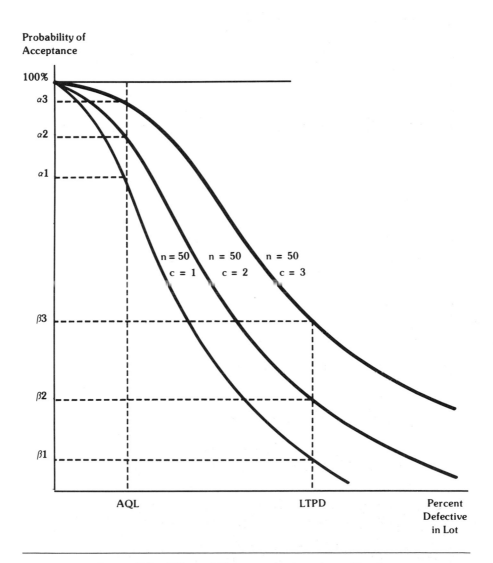

Probability of
Acceptance

Figure 7-5.   Effect of Changing the Acceptance Number

Batch sampling by variables. If the quality characteristic being inspected, such as weight, temperature, or thickness, is measured on a continuous scale, tolerance limits must be set to distinguish good from bad items. For example, one type of automobile tire may be considered acceptable if it will last 25,000

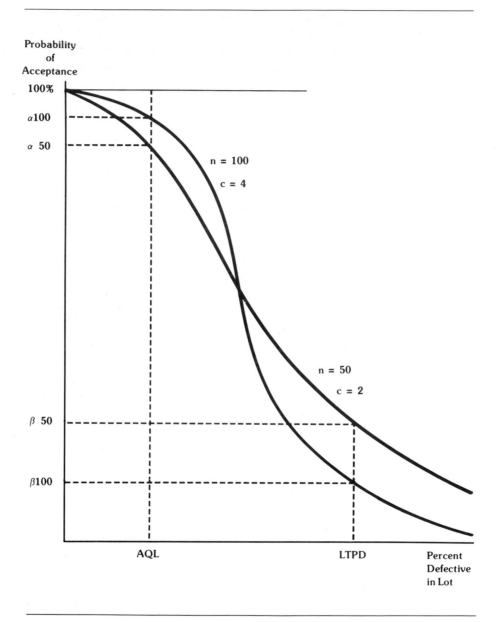

Figure 7-6.   Effect of Changing the Sample Size

miles, plus or minus 3,000 miles. A sample of several tires from the batch could be drawn and tested, and the average mileage in the sample would be used to estimate the percent of tires in the lot that would last 22,000 to 28,000 miles. The lot then would be accepted or rejected based upon that estimate.

Process sampling.   If the item being tested is manufactured continuously rather than in small batches, the problem involves monitoring the process to assure that quality standards are being met. Periodic random samples are taken and plotted on a chart to determine whether the process is "in control" and should continue or is "out of control" and requires corrective action.

Control charts used for this purpose have a line of central tendency (average) and both an upper and lower control limit. These limits generally are set at plus and minus three standard deviations from the mean.

A P-chart (figure 7-7) is used for process sampling by attributes. A random sample is taken from the process, and the percent defective is plotted. As long as the percentage of defects in the sample lies within the control limits, no action is taken. If the sample statistic exceeds either control limit, then the process should be brought back into control.

Process sampling by variables requires monitoring both the mean and the variance of the quality characteristic. The mean of the sample (average weight, for example) is plotted on an $\overline{X}$ ("x bar") chart, illustrated in figure 7-8. Note that the fifth sample taken fell outside the lower control limit, indicating that the average weight of the units may be too light and that a machine adjustment is necessary. Below the $\overline{X}$-chart, the range of the sample is plotted to indicate the variance of the process. A sample outside of control limit on the R-chart would indicate that some units are too heavy and others too light, even though the average is still within acceptable limits.

Applications of Acceptance Sampling

Now we will apply the preceding concepts to the manufacture of the doghouse. Purchased materials—wood, roofing, and chains—would be sampled upon arrival. Each shipment, considered a batch, would be accepted or rejected based on the number of defective items in the sample. Rejected shipments could be returned to the supplier or screened before release to the shop. Some items, like pieces of lumber, could be sampled by attributes; others like the length of the chain, might be sampled by variables.

Within the manufacturing process, either batch or process sampling could be used. Labeling a day's production as a batch, the firm could accept or reject the total amount produced in a day. More likely, it would employ process sampling, using P-charts for attributes, such as missing pieces of trim, and $\overline{X}$ and R charts for variables, such as the size of the door.

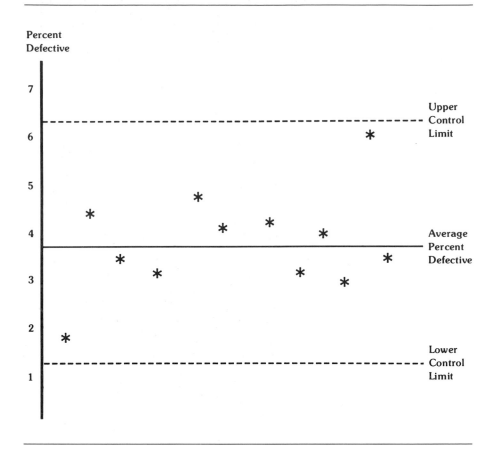

Figure 7-7. P-Chart

The degree of sophistication used—the size and frequency of the samples, as well as the nature of the test—would depend upon estimates and analysis of the relative costs involved.

Organization for Quality Control

The quality-control department in the doghouse manufacturing firm needs the authority and autonomy to perform its job effectively. Because quality is a major company objective, it should not be downgraded by pressures from other company goals of efficiency, quantity, or timeliness of shipments.

When quality control rejects an incoming shipment of materials, adjustments may be necessary in the production schedule or worker assignments.

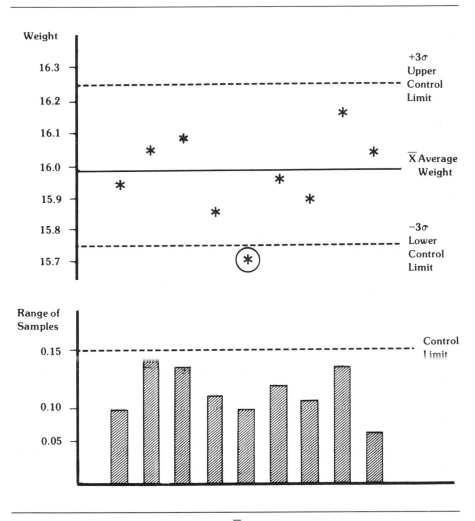

Figure 7-8. $\overline{X}$ and R Chart

A shop foreman who has to wrestle with these problems might prefer to accept and use the unsatisfactory material rather than reschedule, even though the company as a whole might suffer.

It is important, therefore, that quality control be placed at a high position in the organizational structure, preferably reporting directly to the vice-president of manufacturing or the plant manager. If the quality-control manager's decision is to be overridden, it should be done only by someone with the perspective to weigh all ramifications and with the responsibility of bearing the consequences.

The Growing Importance of Quality

Quality always has been an important factor in the production of goods and services, but recent developments have added emphasis and urgency. It is likely that the quality dimension of output will grow in relative importance as firms adjust to changing times.

Consumer advocacy, typified by the work of Ralph Nader, tells organizational leaders what consumers expect. They are tired of products that break, appliances that do not function, and services that are superficial and shoddy. Through both the marketplace and the media, united groups of citizens have found that even the largest organization can be influenced to change the quality of its output.

Consumers also are gaining more strength through new legislation and interpretations of existing legislation relating to product and service liability. Million-dollar lawsuits, which used to be rare, are becoming much more common. The cost of a defect should be weighted against the cost of quality-control efforts to prevent it. Product-liability suits have the effect of pushing up the cost of a defect. Rational decision makers within the firm respond by redoubling their efforts to assure that million-dollar liability defects do not leave the plant. Automobile recalls, food and drug prohibitions, malpractice suits, and scandals in financial institutions indicate that all forms of businesses, private and public, are feeling the pressures.

Increasing foreign and domestic competition merely intensifies the problem. Detroit automobile makers are painfully aware of the quality as well as the cost and style differences between their product and those from Japan or Europe. The U.S. Postal Service is losing business to private delivery services that can provide better service in some urban areas.

In response to these pressures and in anticipation of increasing emphasis in the future, some consumer-product firms have created a new corporate-level executive with the title of vice-president of product integrity. The job involves not only monitoring the manufacture of many products but also working with designers, chemists, industrial engineers, and others who have an impact on the quality of the product. This executive conducts extensive environmental tests on all products and has the power to recall any item considered unsafe, unreliable, or unfair to the consumer.

Emphasis on quality is just one indicator of the recognition of its importance in the ever-changing production function.

References

Crosby, Philip B. *Quality Is Free.* New York: McGraw-Hill, 1979.

Demming, W. Edwards. "Improvement of Quality and Productivity through Action by Management." *National Productivity Review* 1 (Winter, 1981-82): 12-22.

Feigenbaum, Armand V. *Total Quality Control*. 3rd ed. New York: McGraw-Hill, 1983.

Grant, E. L., and Leavenworth, R. S. *Statistical Quality Control*. 5th ed. New York: McGraw-Hill, 1980.

Hostage, B. M. "Quality Control in a Service Business." *Harvard Business Review* 53 (July-August 1975): 98-106.

Juran, J. M. "International Significance of the QC Circle Movement." *Quality Progress* 13 (November 1980): 18-22.

Juran, J. M., and Gryna, F. M. *Quality Planning and Analysis*. 2nd ed. New York: McGraw-Hill, 1980.

Leonard, Frank S., and Sasser, Earl. "The Incline of Quality." *Harvard Business Review* 60 (Sept.-Oct. 1982): 163-171.

Discussion Questions

1. An optimal quality-control policy balances opposing costs. What are the costs involved and the problems of finding the optimal balance in each of the following:
   a. McDonald's Hamburgers?
   b. Grant County Blood Bank?
   c. Southwestern Publishing Company—textbook division?
   d. Gaines Petfood Division?
   e. American Airlines—maintenance division?

2. Our company is planning to introduce a super-deluxe doghouse with lights, air conditioning, windows, and an automatic food and water dispenser. What quality problems would you anticipate?

3. You are the president of a company in a meeting with several of your department heads. The marketing vice-president says that his salespeople have received customer complaints that the quality of the product is not up to that of competitors. Also attending the meeting are the following:
   a. Purchasing Manager—responsible for acquisition of all raw materials and supplies
   b. Personnel Manager—responsible for recruiting, selecting, and training all workers
   c. Plant Engineer—responsible for equipment installation, layout, maintenance, and repair
   d. Plant Supervisor—directs all eight foremen who supervise production workers
   e. Quality-Control Manager—responsible for all incoming, in-process, and final testing and inspection
   What would you tell each of these department heads? Are there others who should be in this meeting? What additional information do you need?

4. Alice wants to take a random sample of the product her department is making to assess its quality. Because she is busy with other things, she decides the easiest strategy is to take four samples: one the first thing in the morning, one as she goes to lunch, one when she returns from lunch, and one just before she leaves to go home. What problems do you see with this plan?

5. A customer complained that the switch on our lawn edger is faulty. The salesperson explained that the switch is a purchased part. Since we do not manufacture it, we cannot control its quality. The customer, not satisfied with that answer, wrote a formal letter of complaint to the president. What letter would you write in response?

6. Five dimensions of quality were discussed. Do any or all of these dimensions apply to a service business, as a car wash or a pizza parlor? Explain.

7. Another dimension of quality that could be added to the list is "consistency," which refers to how well all units of a product conform to the standard. Is this dimension more or less important in service businesses then it is in manufactured products? Explain, using several examples.

8. Which is more important in affecting quality, technical factors or behavioral factors? Concisely explain the relationship between the two.

9. The various costs associated with quality tend to change as the environment changes. Which of these costs is likely to increase in the future, and which is likely to decline? What effect will this have on the optimal quality program?

10. If you were buying a bicycle and had a choice between one that cost $50 but fell apart at the end of one year or a different model that cost $200 but lasted five to ten years, which one would you buy? Why? Which one is higher quality?

Glossary/Index

ABC Analysis: (pages 123, 150) Arrangement of activities—for example, total dollars spent for purchase of particular items—in descending dollar value, so that resources (time) can be allocated according to the relative importance of each activity.

Acceptable Quality Level (AQL): (187) The percent of defects in a lot that would be acceptable most of the time.

Acceptance Number: (186) The maximum number of defects allowed in a sample for acceptance of a lot.

Acceptance Sampling: (186) Inspection of a sample in order to predict the number of defects present in the entire lot. (*See* Batch Sampling *and* Process Sampling.)

Aggregate Planning: (89) The broad, overall decisions which relate to the programming of resources for production over an established time horizon.

Alpha Error: (187) In quality control, for a given sample plan, the percent of times a good lot is rejected. (*See* Type I Error.)

Approved List: (131) List of those vendors who have been evaluated and estimated to be capable of satisfactory performance.

Assembly-Flow Process Chart: (66) A composite of several related process charts showing the work flow for the different purchased and manufactured parts in an assembly operation.

Attributes: (185) In quality control, refers to dichotomous characteristics that make each unit either good or bad (defective).

Attributes Sampling: (186) Quality sampling where the characteristic is measured on a dichotomous basis, such as good/bad.

197

Automated Batch Manufacturing Systems (ABMS):   (60)   A system of several individual machines that process parts into finished units while carried through the system attached to pallets.

Batch Sampling: (186)   Inspection of a sample from a lot in order to accept or reject the entire lot.

Beta Error: (187)   In quality control, for a given sample plan, the percent of times a bad lot is accepted. (*See* Type II Error.)

Bill of Materials: (39, 43, 126, 163)   A list of all items and materials, including the quantities of each, that are required to produce one unit of a finished product or service.

Blank-Check Purchase Order: (136)   Purchase agreement in which vendor is sent a signed, blank check. (After shipment, the vendor enters amount due on the check and deposits it.)

Blanket Order: (136)   Purchase agreement with a vendor to provide the supply of an item for a fixed time period, normally one year.

Breakdown Repair: (61)   Maintenance work undertaken only after the equipment malfunctions or breaks down.

Break-Even Analysis: (50)   Determination of production volume where sales revenue equals the total of variable and fixed costs.

Buffer Stock: (147)   *See* Decoupling Stock *and* Safety Stock.

Capacity Requirements Planning: (93)   A technique providing an integrated approach to estimating future needs in terms of manufacturing capability.

Carrying Costs: (149)   Those costs incurred because something is being stored and not currently used. (The cost is proportional to the number or quantity of the item stored. Typical carrying costs reflect the value of the space occupied by the stored item, the value of the funds tied up in the stock, and insurance costs to protect the stock.)

Cash Discount: (137)   Discount, normally 2 percent, granted if payment is made to vendor within a limited time, normally ten days.

Cellular Layout: (55)   Arrangement of several machines into a miniature product layout for a family of parts.

Centralized Purchasing: (117)   System in which all purchase decisions must be made, and all purchase orders released, by the purchasing agent or department.

Competitive Bid: (134)   Offer to sell, at a price, made by a vendor.

Computer-Aided Design (CAD): (10, 36) A design technique where the computer is used to instantaneously draw pictures on a television screen of what an engineer has designed.

Computer-Aided Manufacturing (CAM): (10, 60) Use of a preprogrammed tool path to provide direct numerical control in the operation of equipment.

Computer Information Exchange: (140) Transmission of data between a firm's purchasing data base and a supplier's data base through a telecommunications system.

Consumer's Risk: (187) *See* Beta Error.

CPM: (97) Acronym for the critical path method, a network modeling technique used to plan and control large-scale projects.

Cycle Counting: (169) A method of checking inventory levels and records on a routine basis—for example, verifying 2 percent of all stock items each week, with some important items being checked more than once a year. (This approach avoids the disruptive effects of the annual "physical" inventory.)

Cycle Stock: (152) The active portion of inventory—that is, the quantity that is depleted, resupplied, depleted, and resupplied again and again. (Cycle stock does not include the quantity known as safety stock.)

Cyclical Component: (87) Time-series variations that are periodic in nature, extending over a period of years, and cannot be expected to repeat themselves with predictable regularity.

Decoupling Stock: (147) That inventory used to isolate sequential operations from one another so that they can be performed independently.

Dependent Demand: (163) *See* Internal Demand.

Detailed Scheduling: (94) Matching the job and resource flows required to meet the master schedule requirements on a time scale.

Durability: (176) The ability of a product to function under adverse conditions.

Economic Lot Size: (154) The number of units put into production to minimize the combined costs of setups and carrying inventory over a specified planning period, usually a year.

Economic Order Quantity: (150) The number of units purchased at one time to minimize the combined costs of ordering material and storing the inventory over a specified planning period, usually a year.

Effectiveness: (19) The degree to which the organization's goals or purposes are achieved.

Efficiency: (19)   The relative amount of resources and time consumed in the production of output.

Element: (74)   A subdivision of a task. (Elements are used in the analysis of work.)

Elemental Data: (74)   Tables of time values based on cataloging repetitive elements common to similar types of work.

Energy Management Program (EMP):   (62)   A program designed to control and reduce energy requirements.

Escalation/De-Escalation: (135)   Purchase contract clause in a long-term agreement which provides that price automatically increases or decreases if a specific economic change, e.g., a basic steel price increase, occurs.

Expediting: (137)   In purchasing, putting pressure on a vendor to assure that the original delivery promise is met or to get earlier delivery. (In production, it means changing the priority of a problem job so that it or other jobs may progress more smoothly through subsequent operations.)

Exponential Smoothing: (84)   A mathematical forecasting model that uses past forecasts and forecast errors to make a new forecast.

External Demand: (82)   Demand unrelated to the demands for other items produced by the firm; also called independent demand.

Extrinsic Models: (87)   Forecasting techniques that attempt to determine how variables (independent variables) external to the variable being predicted relate to this dependent variable.

Fixed Path Equipment: (58)   Relatively inflexible equipment (conveyors, chutes, cranes, and hoists) that handles materials in large volume, normally in a continuous flow.

Fixed-Position Layout: (55)   Due to weight or bulk of the product being manufactured, it remains in one position while workers, tools, and materials move to it.

Flow Diagram: (66)   Symbols connected by arrows on a floor plan to depict the flow of the work process.

Flow-Process Chart: (66)   Use of standard symbols to chart the sequence, distance, and time involved in the flow of work.

Flow Process Production: (18)   Continuous flow manufacturing, where the output is not in discrete units. Petroleum refining is an example of flow process production.

Follow-up of Purchase Order: (136)   Routine checking on the status of a purchase to determine if the vendor will be able to meet the required delivery date.

Forecast Horizon: (82) The time period over which the forecast is to be developed.

Foreign Purchasing: (141) Purchase by U.S. firms of goods from vendors outside North America.

Fork Truck: (58) Special mechanized truck fitted with a hoisting mechanism to transport and stack pallet loads.

Forward Buying: (125) Purchase of a larger-than-normal quantity, due to anticipated shortage or price increase.

Functionality: (175) The degree to which a product or service performs the function for which it was designed.

Group Layout: (55) *See* Cellular Layout.

Group Technology: (55, 162) An approach to manufacturing which groups families of products in order to gain planning and manufacturing economies.

Hand-to-Mouth Buying: (125) Purchase of a smaller-than-normal quantity, due to anticipated market oversupply or price decrease.

Hueristic: (91) A rule-of-thumb approach developed and utilized as a guide to solving problems and making decisions.

Independent Demand: (82, 163) *See* External Demand.

Intermittent Production: (18) Producing in lot sizes larger than in a job shop but smaller than in repetitive production.

Internal Demand: (81) Demand derived from or contingent upon the demand for an end product or other item; also called dependent demand.

Interstation Analysis: (65) Charting of the flow of work performed by individuals at various work stations. The five commonly used charts are the flow-process chart, assembly-flow chart, flow diagram, operation process chart, and office process flow chart.

Intrastation Analysis: (68) Charting of work performed by one person at one location, using a worker-and-machine chart, multiple-activity chart, or operation analysis.

Intrinsic Models: (83) Forecasting techniques that use only the past history of the variable to be projected; commonly called time-series models.

Job Shop: (17) Produces output in small lot sizes or batches, such as a print shop.

Judgmental Models: (83) Forecasting techniques that use expert opinion regarding anticipated happenings to predict future occurrences.

Just-in-Time (JIT) Inventory Systems: (10, 161) Computerized scheduling of materials to arrive just as they are needed, in order to minimize inventory investment.

Kanban: (162) A card system originating in Japan for coordinating the flow of materials on the shop floor.

Layout: (14, 52) The arrangement of machines, equipment, materials handling, aisles, service areas, storage areas, and work stations within the facility.

Lead Time: (157) The period (days, months) needed to replenish stocks once that need has been recognized.

Line Balancing: (57) Arranging each step in the process within a product type layout to provide equal capacity so that material flow will be uninterrupted.

Loading: (93) Assigning jobs to a work center, usually in terms of the labor content of the jobs relative to the labor capacity of the work center.

Lot-sizing: (164) Determining the number of units to manufacture in one batch. (*See* Economic Lot Size.)

Lot Tolerance Percent Defective (LTPD): (187) The percent of defects in a lot that would make it unacceptable most of the time.

Make or Buy: (128) Consideration of cost, quality, and delivery time and reliability factors to determine whether a particular item should be made in house or should be purchased from a vendor.

Master Schedule: (91) A macro-type planning tool that indicates how much of each item is to be produced and when it will be available.

Material/Sales Ratio: (111) Percent of the sales dollar spent for materials, supplies, and services needed to build a product or create a service.

Materials Management: (119) Organizational concept in which a single manager has authority and responsibility for all activities principally concerned with the flow of materials into an organization. (Purchasing, production planning and scheduling, incoming traffic, inventory control, receiving, and stores normally are included.)

Materials Requirements Planning: (101, 163) *See* MRP.

Memo-motion: (70) A special camera analysis technique utilizing only 50 to 100 frames per minute; used in work-study activities.

Methodology (of Transformation): (5) Management principles and techniques, such as planning, forecasting, scheduling, and controlling, involved in transforming inputs into outputs.

Microchronometer: (70) Special clock used for accurate and detailed analysis of a worker's hand motions.

Micromotion Study: (70) A detailed analysis of hand motions by means of a movie camera and standard symbols.

Minority Vendor Program: (129) Conscious action by the purchasing department to locate, develop, and buy from firms owned by minority citizens.

Modular Design: (35) Designing products with easily detachable sections, or modules.

MRO: (123) Maintenance, repair, and operating supplies (as distinguished from raw material or capital equipment).

MRP: (101, 163) Acronym for materials requirements planning, a technique providing an integrated approach to scheduling.

Negotiation: (134) Arriving at an agreement on the essentials of a purchase contract, through discussion between buyer and seller.

Numerical Control (N/C) Machines: (59) Equipment preprogrammed in order to follow a cycle of operations repetitively without human intervention.

Occupational Safety and Health Act (OSHA): (63) Legislation passed by Congress incorporating sanctions designed to improve employee safety and health.

Office Process Flow Chart: (68) Depicts the chronological flow of multiple copies and accompanying operations in paperwork systems.

One-Time Order Quantities: (160) A method of order sizing when reordering during the life of the product is impossible.

Operating Characteristics Curve: (186) For each quality control sample plan, the curve that shows the probability of acceptance of a lot relative to the percent defective in the lot.

Operation Chart: (70) Uses symbols to depict how a worker uses each hand during the work cycle at an individual work station.

Operation Process Chart: (66) Shows the work flow in an assembly operation, using only two symbols—operation and inspection.

Operations Research: (10, 50) The use of quantitative tools—for example, simulation—to structure and analyze a problem in order to reach a mathematically optimal solution.

Ordering Costs: (148) Those fixed costs associated with placing a purchase order, regardless of the dollars or number of units represented in the order.

P-Chart: (191) Plots the percent defective (attributes) of samples taken from a continuous process.

Pallet Loads: (58) Loads of materials placed upon a platform base to facilitate handling of multiple packages and heavy loads by means of mechanical handling equipment such as fork trucks or stacking cranes.

Performance Rating: (73) Evaluation of the employee effort or pace against normal performance or normal pace (100 percent).

PERT: (97) Acronym for the program evaluation and review technique; a network modeling technique used to plan and control large-scale projects.

Pilot Production Run: (39) Manufacture of a small quantity of a new product under simulated normal production conditions to determine any product defects or process inefficiencies that may still exist.

Plant Visit: (130) Inspection and evaluation of a vendor's facility, normally done prior to purchase of the vendor's products.

Predetermined Motion-Time Study: (74) A form of synthetic time standard based upon tables of data developed through use of motion picture cameras or special electronic timing equipment.

Preventive Maintenance (PM): (61) A program of scheduled maintenance designed to reduce the likelihood of equipment breakdown.

Process Charts: (65) Diagrams which depict the flow of work through use of special symbols. (These are used to analyze the present work flow, as the first step in work design; *see also* Flow-Process Chart.)

Process Layout: (53) Arrangement of work facilities based on grouping together similar-type equipment.

Process Sampling: (191) Inspection of a sample from an ongoing process to see if corrective actions are needed.

Producer's Risk: (187) *See* Alpha Error.

Product: (27) The tangible output of the production process.

Product Layout: (53) Arrangement of work and equipment so that material flows according to the progressive steps by which the product is made.

Product Life Cycle: (28) The five steps through which a product passes during its life: introduction, growth, maturity, saturation, and decline.

Production Function: (2) The process of transforming inputs (material, equipment, effort, energy) into outputs (products and services).

Production Scheduling: (91) Determination of the sequence and timing of manufacturing activities.

Productivity: (20)   The ratio of outputs to inputs—material, labor, capital, and energy. (Output-per-man-hour often is used to measure productivity.)

Profit-Leverage Effect of Purchasing: (114)   A dollar saved by better purchasing has the same effect on profits as a sales increase of many (ten to twenty) times that amount.

Progress Control: (96)   Constant monitoring of jobs, as they pass through a facility, to assure that all manufacturing requirements are being met.

Project Production: (18)   Manufacture of items when only one or a very few complex units are produced. (Shipbuilding is an example of project production.)

Purchase Lead Time: (125)   Normal elapsed time from the date a need is recognized until the required item is received from a vendor.

Purchase Order: (135)   Legal document that spells out the quantity, quality, delivery date, price, and conditions of the purchase of items from a vendor.

Purchasing/Materials Management Strategy: (141)   Long-term (5 to 20 years) planning of purchase actions.

Quality: (174)   Characteristics of a product or service that determine its value in the marketplace and how well it performs the function for which it was designed.

Quality Circle: (182)   A group of workers who meet together weekly to discuss problems of quality, or other factors, and develop solutions.

Quality Costs: (182, 194)   Costs associated with improving quality (such as better equipment) and costs associated with poor quality (such as returned items).

R-Chart: (191)   Plots the range of a sample characteristic (variable) taken from a continuous process; *see also* X-bar Chart.

Random Component: (84)   Variations in time-series data that have no regular pattern or change over brief periods of time; also called irregular or noise influences.

Receipt and Inspection of Goods: (137)   Verification that quantity and quality of items received from a vendor agree with the purchase specifications.

Reliability: (176)   How long a product functions under normal conditions.

Reorder Point: (157)   Stock level that signals the inventory controller to start the reordering process because there is only enough stock to meet normal needs during the resupply lead time and still have the desired safety stock available.

Repetitive Production: (17) Manufacturing many units of the same product with a unit moving through each state of the process as that operation is completed—for example, an automobile assembly line.

Research and Development: (13, 29) Those activities principally concerned with investigation directed toward discovering new scientific knowledge (research) and translating this new knowledge into marketable goods and services (development).

Return-on-Assets: (114) Measurement of the productivity of assets employed by a firm; computed by multiplying investment turnover times profit margin.

Robinson-Patman Act: (132) Federal law requiring that a vendor charge all buyers the same price for the same item purchased in the same quantity.

Robot: (60) Equipment that is computer controlled and designed to replace the human operator.

Route Sheet: (41) Lists the sequence of operations necessary to start from material inputs (shown in the bill of materials) through production of the finished product.

Safety Stock: (147, 157) That inventory used to protect against running out of supplies due to late delivery from suppliers or unusually high usage during the resupply period.

Sample Plan: (186) The number of units to be sampled from a lot, and the number of defects that determines acceptance or rejection.

Sample Size: (186) The number of units sampled from a lot of material.

Sampling: (75, 186, 191) *See* Work Sampling, Acceptance Sampling, Batch Sampling, *and* Process Sampling.

Screening: (185) Inspection of *every* unit in a lot.

Seasonal Component: (86) Time-series variations that are periodic and can be expected to recur regularly within a certain period, usually one year or less.

Seasonal Inventories: (146) Items produced and stored to meet high demand in a later period.

Service: (28) Something that satisfies a customer's need without providing that customer with a tangible product.

Service Level Policy: (158) The policy that defines the percent of time that an item can be out of stock.

Setup Costs: (148)   Incurred when a system is rearranged to perform a different task—for example, changing a TV studio set in preparation for taping a different series. (The cost is independent of the number of times the new arrangement will be used.)

Sherman Anti-Trust Act: (132)   Makes any combination, collusion, or conspiracy by sellers or buyers to set price or restrict trade illegal.

Single Sourcing: (139)   Purchase of all requirements of a given item from only one vendor, even though several vendors could supply it.

Specifications: (13, 39, 43)   The detailed description of a product or service, usually including a list of measurable characteristics, the different parts or materials that go into a product or service, and often a detailed set of directions of how to assemble the product or properly perform the service.

Stacking Crane: (58)   A device which lifts pallet loads vertically and horizontally for placement within very high storage rack areas.

Standardization: (34, 109)   The process of establishing agreement on uniform identifications for certain characteristics of quality, design, performance, quantity, and service. (An agreed-upon uniform identification is called a standard.)

Statistical Quality Control (SQC):   (184)   The use of probability theory and statistical principles to determine quality sampling procedures.

Stock-keeping Unit (SKU):   (168)   One unit of an item—for example, a given size or color—in a particular location.

Strategic Material Planning: (108, 141)   Long-term forecast of demand, supply, and price of key raw materials to identify potential problems. Based on forecast results, alternative action courses are formulated.

Technology (of Transformation):   (5)   Scientific principles applied to convert inputs into outputs, such as the chemistry and physics involved in petroleum refining.

Therblig: (70)   A fundamental movement or action—for example, transport, load, grasp, or hold—used in constructing detailed motion charts for the analysis of hand movements.

Thomas Register of American Manufacturers: (128)   Widely-used directory listing United States manufacturers by type of item produced.

Time-Series Models: (83)   *See* Intrinsic Models.

Time Study: (73)   Work measurement technique which normally uses a stopwatch to determine the time required to do a job. (The analyst then uses a performance rating, to allow for normal delays, to determine a standard time.)

Total Quality Control (TQC):   (176, 179)   An organizational approach to the strategic management of quality in all phases of the design and manufacturing process.

Transfer Machines: (54, 60)   Provision for the automatic transfer of material between machines for continuous processing.

Transportation Deregulation: (140)   Removal of restrictions regarding service and rates for movement of goods by carriers.

Travel Chart: (57)   Records the frequency of loads between departments, providing information for potential rearrangements.

Travelling Requisition: (126)   Used to notify purchasing of a need to purchase. (This form can be used for up to thirty-six buys, and it moves back and forth between requisitioner and purchasing without requiring repeated copying of routine information.)

Trend Component: (86)   Long-term variations in time series.

Type I Error: (187)   Rejecting a lot that should have been accepted; also called an "alpha error" or "producer's risk."

Type II Error: (187)   Accepting a lot that should have been rejected; also called a "beta error" or "consumer's risk."

Value Analysis: (33)   The organized and systematic study of every element of cost in a material, part, or service to ensure that it fulfills its function at the lowest total cost.

Variable: (185)   In quality control, a characteristic measured on a continuous scale, such as temperature, length, or color.

Variables Sampling: (189)   Quality sampling where the characteristic is measured on a continuous scale such as length, temperature, or weight.

Varied Path Equipment: (58)   Flexible equipment (such as a forklift truck) that normally handles equipment in lots.

Vendor: (128)   An outside supplier of raw materials, supplies, or services needed in the operation of an organization.

Vendor Directory: (128)   Volume that lists vendors and their addresses, arranged by product.

Vendor Point Rating System: (131)   Method of evaluating vendor performance in which points are assigned to how well the vendor performed on several factors, such as quality, delivery, and price.

Wage Incentive: (64, 76)   Plan whereby an individual or group receives additional pay, a bonus, or profit sharing based on performance in relation to a work standard established through work measurement.

Work Design: (14, 64)   Systematic approach to finding the most effective and efficient method of doing a job; also known as methods study or motion study.

Work Distribution Chart: (70)   A summary of the activities and tasks performed by a group.

Work Measurement: (14, 64, 73)   Determination of how long it should take a qualified and trained employee working at a normal pace to do a specific task or operation, with due allowances for fatigue and personal and unavoidable delays; also known as time study.

Work Sampling: (75)   The application of probability theory involving random observations to determine the time distribution within a given work activity.

Work Study: (64)   The utilization of work design to establish and improve work procedures and methods, coupled with a work measurement system that facilitates usable work standards for planning and controlling operations.

Worker-and-Machine Chart: (68)   Depicts against a time scale the respective activity of one or more persons operating one or more machines.

X-bar Chart: (191)   Plots the mean of a characteristic (variable) for a sample taken from a continuous process; *see also* R-Chart.

Zero Inventory: (161)   The conceptual goal of the Japanese to operate a manufacturing facility with as close to zero inventory as possible.